Collins **Revision**

GCSE Citizenship

Edexcel

Revision guide

Jenny Wales

Contents

Revision Guide

Contents

How to use this Revision Guide

Your GCSE Citizenship Studies course

You can study Citizenship Studies as either a short course or a full GCSE.

If you are doing the short course, you need to know all about the material for Unit 1: Citizenship Today and Unit 2: Participating in Society.

If you are doing the full course, you will add Unit 3: Citizenship in Context and Unit 4: Citizenship Campaign.

This book will help you revise for Units 1 and 3, which are assessed by exams. You will find a mix of different sorts of questions in each exam. The book has all sorts of guidance and tips to help you to do your best.

The book does not give revision help on Units 2 or 4, as they are projects that you complete and they are not assessed by exams.

How will this Guide help?

There is a variety of questions in the exams for Units 1 and 3. This Guide can help you revise so that you can tackle the different sorts of questions. Here are some examples.

The multiple-choice and short-answer questions

To answer questions like this, you have to know your stuff. Every section in the Revision Guide starts with a section called 'Know the facts'. This contains all the facts you need to know for that section. Here are some examples of the questions and the 'facts' that will help you to answer them.

contract of employment

a document that details an employee's and employer's responsibilities for a particular job

representative democracy

a type of democracy where citizens have the right to choose someone to represent them on a council or in Parliament as an MP

pressure group

a group of people that tries to change public opinion or government policy to its own views or beliefs

What is a contract of employment?

A A statement listing an employer's and employee's responsibilities concerning a job.

B An agreement in which an employer instructs an employment agency to recruit a new member of staff for the employer.

C An agreement between an employer and a union about the number of people to be employed.

D An agreement between individuals and their trade union. *1 mark*

What is the difference between a political party and a pressure group? *2 marks*

You will find some examples of questions like this in the section called 'In the exam', which looks like this:

In the exam

Questions based on issues

Almost every question is based on source material that presents an account about an issue. In both the Unit 1 and Unit 3 exams you will be expected to look carefully at the source material to help you to answer the questions. The sources are about issues concerning the world at large, such as human rights or why we need laws. In each section of the book you will find a section entitled 'What are the issues?' It highlights the main issues that arise from each topic in the course, so you will have some idea of the sort of questions to expect in the exams.

What are the issues?

Don't forget

You will often come across a heading in the margin that gives you a hint about things that people often get wrong – or ways of doing things better. Here's an example:

Extended writing

In the Unit 1 exam you will need to choose one longer question, from a choice of three. Look at each one carefully and decide which you can do best. Take a few minutes because there is quite a lot to take in. Remember to look at the bullet points, which are designed to help you structure your writing.

Raising your grade

In the 'Raising your grade' sections of this book you will find 'Exam tips'. These give you some hints on producing a good answer. Here's an example.

The key to getting a good mark here is to make sure you put both sides of the argument and then to come to a conclusion that you can support with facts and evidence. To help you to learn how to do this, every section has a feature that does just this – 'On one hand' and 'On the other hand'. Here is an example.

Don't forget!

The European Parliament is not the main decision making body of the EU. The Council of Ministers makes the decisions.

Exam tip

If you can see good reasons for both sides of the argument – debate the two but make sure you come to a conclusion – even if you want to explain your reservations.

On one hand

- The UN Declaration on Human Rights sets the standards.
- Most countries abide by it.
- It organizes peace keeping missions when countries fight each other – or within countries.
- It co-ordinates disaster relief. It would be difficult for other organizations to do this.

On the other hand

- Many countries ignore the UNDHR.
- The UN does not pass laws so it has no power.
- There are other organizations like the EU and the Commonwealth which could take the role.

At the end of each 'Raising your grade' section you will find part of an answer written by a student like yourself.

We have picked out some good points in each answer and explained why they are good. They are set out so that you can see exactly what to do yourself. Here are three examples:

The first sentence sets out the student's point of view very clearly.	I believe that everyone should take both their rights and their responsibilities seriously.
A good practical example. This shows that the student has made the connections between real, local events and Citizenship.	A supermarket chain wanted to build a new store near where I live...
Having set a very good case, the student now needs to put the other side of the argument. 'On the other hand…' tells the examiner that the other side is coming next.	On the other hand...

What skills do you need?

The Citizenship Studies course asks you to use a range of skills in both learning and in answering the questions. You will get lots of practice at working out how to do things and making decisions about the best course of action while doing your Citizenship Activity in Unit 2. All these skills will help you in the exams, too.

Here are some ways that you can put your skills to work.

Know what's going on

Citizenship Studies is all about what's going on in the world – so make sure you keep in touch with things going on in your local community as well as the big issues that affect us all. This will help you to get used to thinking about the issues that are likely to come up in the exams.

Know the facts

The source material that you will use in the exams is full of ideas that you will need to recognise and be able to define. It is therefore important to know the facts that are given in the fact boxes in every section. Here are two examples:

Explain the facts

Questions will expect you to know the facts – and to be able to explain them. During your course you will have used the facts in different situations and this will help you to explain them. In each section of the book you are asked to write a sentence that shows you understand each fact. This is good practice for the 'explain' questions in the exams. Draw up a table like the one below so you can practise the definition and the explanation.

civil law

this covers disputes between individuals or groups. Civil law cases are often about rights

jury

a group of people who decide if someone is guilty in a court of law

Fact	Definition	Explanation
Rate of inflation	The rate at which prices rise	When prices rise, the value of money falls, so borrowers win and savers lose.

Give examples

In both the short answer questions and the extended writing, you are often asked to give examples. If you know what's going on, you will probably have lots of examples at hand to help you answer these questions. Examples might be local, national or international. They will need to be convincing for an examiner who does not know your local area. Look at the pictures as you go through the book because they often offer you the examples that you might need.

Working with source material

Here is a taste of the sort of material that you might be asked to work with. It is all based on stories that are in the news. Remember that the papers are set about 18 months before the exams take place, so you need to be following the news from the beginning of your course. There will often be a mix of words, pictures and some data. The numbers aren't scary – you just need to be able to make your knowledge work to interpret them.

Make sure you read the source material carefully before you begin.

Here is an example:

Full body scanners introduced at airports

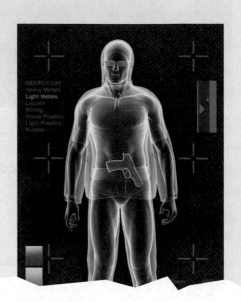

Full body scanners at Heathrow and Manchester airports have caused outrage among civil liberty campaigners. They claim the scanners, which act like a mini radar device 'seeing' beneath ordinary clothing, break the Human Rights Act.

Another point of view

You will have practised this over and over again – because if you don't put another point of view, you can't get more than half marks in the long questions. When you are doing the long questions in the exam, start by writing down your two different points of view in two lists. This will guide your writing and help you to get going.

Now you are ready to start your revision for Citizenship GCSE.

1.1 Community and identity

You will revise

• **How people develop their identities** • **How communities work** •

Know the facts

In the exam you will be asked questions to test your knowledge of the key facts, so it is really important to learn them. Write a sentence for each of the key facts to show you understand what they mean. You will need to use an example in each sentence, so if you can't think of one – go and look it up!

community	**neighbourhood**	**British nationals**
a group of people who are in close contact and who share common interests and values	a local area within which people live as neighbours, sharing living space and interests	citizens of the United Kingdom

multicultural community	**cultural diversity**	**dual heritage**
a community made up of people from many different cultural or ethnic groups	the range of different groups that make up a wider population	people with parents or recent ancestors of different origins

emigration	**immigration**	**minority**
leaving your homeland to move to another country	moving to another country to live there	a small part of a larger group of people

identity	**identity card**	**tolerant**
who or what someone or something is	a card that establishes someone's identity	open-minded, accepting

What are the issues?

Think about

Look carefully at the data. Is it what you expect? Think about how it affects communities.

Where do we all come from?

The UK population: the mix (millions)			
White	42.7	Pakistani	0.8
Black Caribbean	0.6	Bangladeshi	0.3
Black African	0.6	Chinese	0.3
Indian	1.2	Other groups	0.3

Source: Social Trends 2008, ONS

How have the patterns of migration changed – and why?

What reasons do people have for leaving their home country and coming to the UK?

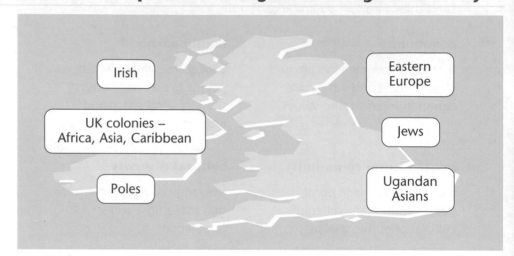

Irish

UK colonies –
Africa, Asia, Caribbean

Poles

Eastern Europe

Jews

Ugandan Asians

How diverse are our religious beliefs?

Think of as many examples as you can of the effect of religious diversity in the UK.

Many people in the UK claim to be Christians but there are many people with other religious beliefs:

- Bangladeshis are mostly Muslim, with a small number of Hindus
- Indians from the Punjab are mostly Sikh, with some Hindus
- Indians from Gujarat are mostly Hindus, with some Muslims
- Pakistanis are usually Muslim
- Chinese are usually Christian, Confucian or Buddhist
- Black Caribbeans are usually Christian or Rastafarian.

How do people come to have multiple identities?

What identities do you have? Do any of your identities lead you to disagree with people? Do any help you to get on with people? Think of examples of identity that might help people to get on.

How has society in the UK changed and how does it continue to change?

- The number of work applications from the new member countries of the EU dropped to 29,000 in the last three months of 2008, down from 53,000 in the same period of 2007. Research suggested that many of those that came have now gone home.

- The majority of workers from Eastern Europe are young – 78 per cent are aged 18–34 – and only 11 per cent had brought dependants with them to work in Britain.

- Only 3,860 refugees were granted the right to settle in Britain in 2008, down from 67,000 in 2005.

What sorts of communities are living together in the UK?

Communities mix in different ways in different parts of the UK. Some areas have a considerable mix of different communities but in other areas there may only be one or two.

What is the effect of changes in cultural diversity?

Nearly all adults eat at least one ethnic style of food, with just over three in ten consuming five or more styles. Enjoyment of ethnic food is greatest with young adults – with just over seven in ten of those aged 25–44.

How does this diversity affect community cohesion and integration?

'Pakistanis and Bangladeshis are easily the poorest group in Britain. They are significantly poorer than white pensioners. There are serious pockets of disadvantage in other minority groups too, especially among young men and women of Caribbean origin. Other results of the survey suggests that minority groups can and will achieve prosperity in multicultural Britain, but policies to address racial disadvantage are still urgently needed.'

Ethnic Minorities in Britain: diversity and disadvantage 2009

Think about

What changes does this information suggest have taken place in the UK? What other factors do you think have affected the way we live?

Describe the mix of people in your school or town. How do people's opinions affect their views of their community?

The food we eat is just one product of our cultural diversity. Are there more serious ways we can grow to understand each other?

Why is it more difficult to achieve community cohesion when some communities are very poor?

In the exam

1 Explain what is meant by immigration. *2 marks*

2 Which of the following describe a community? *1 mark*

   A Passengers on a railway journey.

   B People who bought a house in the same year.

   C People who live in the same village.

   D Everyone who suffers from diabetes.

3 A multicultural community is one in which: *1 mark*

   A everyone enjoys cultural activities such as ballet and opera

   B there are many small businesses

   C there are people of all age groups

   D there are people from many different cultural and ethnic groups.

Don't forget!

Less than 10 per cent of the UK population belongs to ethnic minorities. Many students think this figure is much higher.

Raising your grade

'Britain is a multicultural country, so people should not try to live in separate communities.'

Do you agree with this view?

Give reasons for your opinion, showing you have considered another point of view. You should support your argument with examples wherever possible.

- Why do you think people might want to live in separate communities?
- Why does it matter if people want to live separate lives?
- How might it help if everyone goes to the same school?
- What advantages are there if people from different cultures mix together?

On one hand

If people live together:

- they learn about each other's cultures
- they are less likely to fall out
- the children grow up together at school
- they widen their experiences – like eating different food.

On the other hand

If people live in separate communities:

- they might be afraid of people in other communities
- they do not learn English and find it hard to find work
- the children might grow apart from their parents because they go to school and mix with other communities.

Here's the final paragraph of an A-grade answer.

I believe that people should not lead separate lives. Although they may come from different backgrounds and speak different languages, it is important that they all feel part of the same community. I understand that people do not want to lose their identities and may be afraid of people who are different but unless we all make an effort to live together, there may be problems. We have seen trouble erupt in towns where communities are living separate lives. It is often because people are scared or feel that things are not fair. Sometimes the media whips up fear about housing and other issues – even when there is no real evidence to back up the story. Despite the difficulties I think people and communities should try hard to work together.

Here the student shows they are aware of issues in the news. This brings their writing to life and shows they can apply the ideas.

Shows another point of view: why people might want to live separately. This raises the grade immediately.

This shows that the student understands the difference between fact and opinion.

1.2 Human, legal and political rights

You will revise

- **What is meant by human rights** • **How they are protected**
- **How the law affects our rights and responsibilities** • **Our political rights** •

Know the facts

In the exam you will be asked questions to test your knowledge of the key facts, so it is really important to learn them. Write a sentence for each of the key facts to show you understand what they mean. You will need to use an example in each sentence, so if you can't think of one – go and look it up!

convention an agreement, often between governments	**declaration** a document setting down aims and intentions	**Act** a law passed by Parliament
human rights things that people are morally or legally allowed to do or have	**legal rights** rights that are protected by law	**political rights** rights to take part in elections and other democratic activities
discrimination treating someone less favourably because of their colour, ethnic origins, gender or disability	**homophobic** fearing or hating homosexuals	**racism** the idea that some people of different origins are not as good as others
respect to have a good opinion of someone	**responsibility** something it is your duty to do or to look after	**inclusive education** schooling that involves everyone, regardless of disability
vote to choose a candidate in an election	**democracy** government by the people, either directly or through elected representatives	**election** selection of one or more people for an official position by voting
member of Parliament a person who has been elected to represent a part of the country in Parliament	**member of the European Parliament** a person who has been elected to represent a part of the country in the European Parliament	**councillor** a member of a local council, elected by people in the area
compensation making amends; something given to make good a loss		

Think about

What are human rights?

What human rights are these children deprived of?

How are they protected?

- United Nations Declaration of Human Rights.
- The Convention on the Rights of the Child (CRC).

What other rights are included in the UN Declaration of Human Rights?

What are legal rights?

There are legal rights affecting education, work, travel, food, health, meeting friends, owning property, religion, marrying, having children, minorities, life, freedom, privacy, fair trial, torture and voting.

Are these all human rights? Do we have laws to protect these rights?

How are people protected from discrimination?

How might this person suffer from discrimination? What other groups of people might suffer discrimination? How does the law protect them?

What are our responsibilities?

Joe rides his bike all over town – but he always wants to get there very quickly! He sometimes jumps the lights and often rides on the pavement. When someone gets in the way, he hurls abuse. Last time he jumped the lights, a car hit him and he ended up in hospital.

Wants and needs?

What you have a right to and what you want is not the same thing. For instance, the Convention on the Rights of the Child states that you have the right to 'clean water and healthy food'. You might say, 'I don't like drinking water. I want Coke or coffee!' But the CRC focuses on the most basic human rights and needs, which are denied to millions of people all over the world: it isn't about 'wants'.

What are our political rights?

'To vote and to be elected at genuine elections which shall be held by secret ballot'

International Covenant of Political Rights

- Locally: we elect councillors.

- Nationally: we elect Members of Parliament.

- Internationally: we elect Members of the European Parliament.

Why is free speech important?

In the UK we are free to say what we like, as long as we don't break the law by discriminating against others or inciting violence.

People can also organize campaigns and meet to protest against activity they don't like. Without these freedoms, our political rights would be meaningless because it would be very difficult to oppose the government or protest against the activities of other organizations.

In the exam

1 What is meant by a political right? *1 mark*

2 What is the difference between an MP and an MEP? *2 marks*

3 Explain what is meant by democracy. Give an example. *2 marks*

Think about

If you ride a bike, what are your responsibilities? How are you protected by the law? How are others protected from you?

Compare your life with the children in the first picture. What do you both need? How do you think your needs and wants compare with your grandparents' needs and wants when they were your age?

How does having your say make a difference to your views on big issues?

Why are political rights meaningless without freedom of speech? Think of a country where people do not have this freedom.

Don't forget!

It is important to be able to distinguish between human and legal rights. Legal rights are part of the law of a country, whereas human rights are a convention or declaration and cannot be enforced.

Raising your grade

'People should never have rights without responsibilities.'

Do you agree with this view?

Give reasons for your opinion, showing you have considered another point of view. You should support your argument with examples wherever possible.

- Why are rights important?
- What happens if people demand their rights but ignore their responsibilities?
- Are there any people who might needs rights more than responsibilities?
- Is everyone aware of their responsibilities?

On one hand

- Rights and responsibilities are two sides of the same coin.
- People need rights to keep them safe.
- People should respect each other.
- Communities can be difficult to live in if people don't take their responsibilities seriously.

On the other hand

- Young children need to be protected by their rights.
- People who can't make decisions for themselves can't be expected to carry out responsibilities.
- If people are unaware of their responsibilities, they cannot be expected to carry them out.

Here's part of an answer from an A-grade candidate.

> I believe that <u>everyone should take both their rights and their responsibilities seriously</u>. It makes living together in communities much easier because people respect each other. If people don't respect each other, they may hurt others or make daily life very difficult.
>
> I agree that rights and responsibilities are two sides of the same coin. <u>You have the right to ride a bike but you have a responsibility to ride it carefully</u> so you don't hurt anyone. People get very upset when young people ride their bikes on the pavement because they might run into young children or older people.
>
> <u>However</u>, in some situations it is unreasonable to expect people to do so. <u>The law says that children under ten are not criminally responsible</u>, so they can't be taken to court if they commit a crime. Even so, children should be learning to take responsibility for their actions from when they are very small. When our responsibilities are spelled out in the law, we must keep them. Not knowing about them is no excuse.

The first sentence sets out the student's point of view very clearly.

Giving an example shows that you understand the idea of rights and responsibilities. It can be an everyday example like this one.

'However' is a very useful word. It means that you are about to put another point of view.

This student shows that they have some useful knowledge that helps to support their argument.

1.3 Development and struggle

You will revise

- **The development of human rights** • **The inequalities that still exist**
- **The struggle that people have had to win the right to vote** •

Know the facts

In the exam you will be asked questions to test your knowledge of the key facts, so it is really important to learn them. Write a sentence for each of the key facts to show you understand what they mean. You will need to use an example in each sentence, so if you can't think of one – go and look it up!

asylum seeker	**suffrage**	**suffragette**
someone who has applied for protection as a refugee and has not yet been told whether they will be accepted	the right to vote	person who campaigned for the right of women to vote

What can people in Europe do if they feel their human rights are being denied?

What are the effects of these inequalities? What can be done about them?

How are human rights protected in Europe?

The European Convention on Human Rights (ECHR) (1950)

This sets the framework for European countries. If the residents of one country don't think they have had a fair response from the courts, they can take their case to the European Court of Human Rights.

The Human Rights Act (1998)

Since 2000, the UK has had its own laws on human rights, which say that all organisations have a duty to protect the rights of all individuals as set out in the ECHR. The Human Rights Act protects everyone in the UK.

Does everyone have their rights?

- Nearly 50 million births are unregistered every year. Nearly half of them live in countries in southern Asia such as India and Bangladesh.

- About 1.2 million children are trafficked worldwide every year.

- More than 250,000 children are currently serving as child soldiers.

- About 72 million children are out of school – many of them are girls.

- About 771 million adults are illiterate.

Does everyone have the right to vote?

Democracy in Afghanistan

Few Afghan women voted in the elections because there were not enough women officials to run the polling stations. Men and women are not allowed to vote in the same place.

Democracy in Zimbabwe

The head of the Pan-African Parliament observer team, who had observed the election in Zimbabwe, said that the current atmosphere of fear prevailing in the country did not give rise to the conduct of free, fair and credible elections.

What rules do you think a country needs to run free and fair elections?

In the exam

1 How can people complain if they feel they are deprived of their human rights?   *1 mark*

2 What is meant by suffrage?   *1 mark*

Don't forget!

Remember that the European Convention on Human Rights influences laws in the UK.

Exam tip

Remember to use the key terms you have learnt during the course to support your argument.

Raising your grade

'I can't be bothered to vote. It never seems to make any difference.'

Do you agree with this view?

Give reasons for your opinion, showing you have considered another point of view. You should support your argument with examples wherever possible.

- People have fought for us all to have the vote so shouldn't we use it?
- If you don't vote, can you complain about what happens?
- Do pressure groups have more effect than political parties?
- Is it better to live in a democratic country than a dictatorship?

On one hand

- 'I think you should vote because it is the main way to have your say.'
- Turnout in elections has been falling.
- If turnout is low, the country is not very democratic.
- Voting is to decide who makes all the decisions. Pressure groups just deal with a single issue.

On the other hand

- Pressure groups seem to have more effect.
- More people might vote if we had proportional representation.
- Politicians never seem to listen to the people once they are elected.
- Politicians should speak to people in a way they understand.

Here's part of an answer from an A-grade candidate.

The first sentence says clearly that the student is about to put another point of view. This makes it easy for the examiner.

Using the term 'manifestos' shows that the student has a good understanding of this part of the course and can use ideas well in their argument.

I have now set out why I think you should vote but many people don't. More people vote in Big Brother than in some elections. Big Brother is fun and keeps people interested. Politicians should try harder to communicate with the voters. Most people don't really understand the issues and therefore can't be bothered to vote. They don't realise how a government's decisions can affect them. If politicians set it out more clearly, people might be more willing to vote. Not many people read the manifestos. Perhaps they could use technology better to tell us what they are going to do. The newspapers often do not help because they turn the news into a message that their readers want to hear – so the important points can be missed.

Lots of people care about particular issues and are not very interested in the big picture. They may support pressure groups but not bother to vote. You can see why – when they see pressure groups making a difference. If they looked carefully at what the parties think, they could choose the party that suits them best.

This student takes things a step further and suggests ways of overcoming the problem of people not voting.

1.4 Rights and responsibilities of consumers, employers and employees

You will revise

- **How the law protects consumers**
- **Rights and responsibilities in the workplace** •

Know the facts

In the exam you will be asked questions to test your knowledge of the key facts, so it is really important to learn them. Write a sentence for each of the key facts to show you understand what they mean. You will need to use an example in each sentence, so if you can't think of one – go and look it up!

consumer

a person who buys goods or services for their own use

Citizens Advice Bureau (CAB)

an organization that offers free advice on consumer and other legal matters

Office of Fair Trading

a government office that can take action against traders who break the law

Trading Standards Department

an official body that enforces consumer-based law

European Union (EU)

a group of 25 countries that work together, e.g. on environmental, social and economic issues

employment laws

laws passed by Parliament and by the EU that set out the rights and responsibilities of employers and employees

pressure groups

a group of people that tries to change public opinion or government policy to its own views or beliefs

trade unions

organizations that look after the interests of a group of employees

contract of employment

a document that details an employee's and employer's responsibilities for a job

employment tribunal

a type of court that deals only with disagreements over employment laws

redundancy

when a person loses their job because the job doesn't need to be done anymore

warning

written or spoken warning given by an employer to an employee if the employer thinks the employee has been breaking the contract of employment

dismissal

when an employer ends an employee's contract of employment ('sacking')

Think about

How does each of these Acts protect the customer? Which Act protects the customer in the pictures? Where can you go for help?

What rights do consumers have?

- The Trade Descriptions Act
- The Sale and Supply of Goods Act
- The Food Safety Act
- The Consumer Protection Act

How can people be exploited at work?

What sort of pressure can be put on people at work?

Exploitation at work can happen in several ways:

- long hours
- dangerous or unhealthy working conditions
- poor pay
- workers not being treated as individuals, with individual needs.

How are people protected?

Why are groups stronger than individuals? What situations can the law help with?

Unions

Employers can be very powerful, so employees started to band together. Groups are always stronger than individuals. They formed trade unions and negotiated with employers to reach fairer agreements on pay and working conditions.

Unions persuade employers and Parliament to adopt fairer and safer working practices. They have been effective pressure groups in looking after the interests of their members.

The Law ...

- The Equal Pay Act
- The Contract of Employment
- The Sex Discrimination Act
- The Race Relations Act
- The Employment Equality Regulations
- The Disability Discrimination Act
- Health and safety laws

What are your responsibilities at work?

Think about

What responsibilities does this person have at work?

What if it all goes wrong at work?

Riam Dean, who has an artificial arm, won her case at an employment tribunal. She claimed that clothes store Abercrombie and Fitch had insisted that she worked in the stock room and not on the shop floor because she didn't fit their image.

Riam received compensation. What does this mean?

In the exam

1 Name a right given to a citizen under the Disability Discrimination Act. *1 mark*

2 What is a contract of employment?

  A A statement listing an employer's and an employee's responsibilities concerning a job.

  B An agreement in which an employer instructs an employment agency to recruit a new member of staff for the employer.

  C An agreement between an employer and a union about the number of people to be employed.

  D An agreement between individuals and their trade union. *1 mark*

3 What is an employment tribunal? *1 mark*

Exam tip

The question asks you to 'support your answer with examples'. Make sure you do, as it shows you understand the issues.

Raising your grade

'Consumers have lots of rights but there is little help to enforce them.'

Do you agree with this view?

Give reasons for your opinion, showing you have considered another point of view. You should support your argument with examples wherever possible.

- How does the law protect consumers?
- Why do many people not know their rights?
- Who can help us enforce our rights?
- Why do we sometimes not bother to use our rights?

On one hand

- There are several laws that protect us.
- There are several organizations that help – usually in every big town.
- It is easy to find out about our rights on the internet.
- If you know the law, it is easy to complain and get a result.

On the other hand

- Many people don't know about their rights because they have never been taught about them.
- People often don't have time to pursue a seller if they don't agree to solve the problem.
- It can be embarrassing to complain.
- The Small Claims Court will give an answer but people are often afraid of the law – and it costs money.

This part of an A-grade candidate's answer shows how to put another point of view.

Although I would complain and know the laws that affect my rights, many people do not. No one explains these things to people, so they must find out for themselves. If they have done a GCSE in Citizenship Studies, they are more likely to know about it. It would be a good idea if the government made more effort to inform people of their rights. Unless you know you have rights, you are not going to use the internet to find out about them. It is hard to argue if you do not know your rights.

If you go back to the shop to complain, you often have to be very determined. The people in the shop often do not want to carry out their responsibilities. If your jumper has shrunk when it was washed, they will tell you that you did not follow the washing instructions – even if you did. It can be hard to get a replacement jumper because of this. It makes people not want to complain.

If all else fails, you have to go to the Small Claims Court. There is a fee for doing this and it takes a lot of time. If businesses are not doing a good job, they will hope that dissatisfied customers won't make the effort to do all this.

The student immediately sets out the argument. This means that they will get more than half marks.

Here we can see how the student uses a good argument to put the other point of view.

It's good to use an example because it shows that you can use the ideas that you have learnt.

This shows that the student realizes the practical issues that justified the argument.

2.1 How the media informs and influences public debate

You will revise

- **The influence of the media** • **Why a free press is important**
- **How the media can be controlled** •

Know the facts

In the exam you will be asked questions to test your knowledge of the key facts, so it is really important to learn them. Write a sentence for each of the key facts to show you understand what they mean. You will need to use an example in each sentence, so if you can't think of one – go and look it up!

media

ways of communicating with large numbers of people

journalist

a person who gathers news and produces reports for the media

editor

the person who is responsible for the content of a newspaper or television or radio programme

spin doctor

someone who tries to get certain stories into the public eye and to make bad news sound better

bias

to favour one thing over another unfairly

libel

writing untrue things about people

censorship

limiting the information given to the general public

press freedom

the ability of the press to give information and express opinion

Press Code

guidelines for the media and journalists about the information they gather and how they obtain and use it

slander

saying incorrect things about people

What effect could this change in The Sun's support have on the way people vote?

How does the media influence debate?

The Sun Backs Blair

The Sun Turns to the Tories

Why does the media influence opinion?

What would you do in these situations? Why is important to be able to tell fact from opinion?

There are lots of trade-offs because newspapers want to make a profit from advertising and selling papers. Read these two examples.

A company that buys lots of advertising space hits the headlines for using child labour in Indonesia. The editor must decide whether or not to run the story and risk losing the large income from the adverts.

A famous celebrity has got into trouble – but no-one can say for sure how much of the story is true. The readers will want to hear about the celebrity and will probably buy the paper that has the story on the front page – especially if there is a big picture.

Why is press freedom important?

Why is there a link between press freedom and democracy?

Countries do not always match exactly but there is a link between press freedom and democracy.

	Press freedom ranking	Democracy ranking
Denmark	1	7
Netherlands	7	4
UK	20	21
USA	20	18
South Africa	33	31
Romania	50	50
Zambia	97	97
Russia	153	107
Iraq	154	116
China	168	136
Iran	172	145

Source: Press Freedom Index 2009, Economist Index of Democracy 2008

How can the media be controlled?

The Press Code states that newspapers *must*:

- avoid prejudice
- give a right to reply to any inaccurate reporting
- respect people's private and family life
- protect confidential sources.

The Press Code states that newspapers *must not*:

- publish inaccurate, misleading or distorted information or pictures
- harass people for information
- intrude on grief or shock
- intrude on children during their schooling
- use hidden bugs to find things out
- make payments to people involved in criminal cases
- profit from financial information
- identify victims of sexual assault.

Think about

Why is the Press Code necessary? How does the law protect people?

In the exam

1 Which of the following newspapers can be described as a 'quality' newspaper?

  A The Sun

  B The Independent

  C The Daily Express

  D The Daily Mail   *1 mark*

2 What is censorship?

  A Trying to get stories in the public eye

  B Making journalists obey the press code

  C Promoting press freedom

  D Limiting the information given to the public   *1 mark*

3 What is the difference between slander and libel?   *2 marks*

Don't forget!

Popular papers used to be called 'tabloids'. Quality newspapers were often called 'broadsheets' because they were bigger. Many papers are now printed in a small format so people distinguish between them with the words 'quality' and 'popular' instead.

Raising your grade

'The media should always be free to say what it thinks.'

Do you agree with this view?

Give reasons for your opinion, showing you have considered another point of view. You should support your argument with examples wherever possible.

- Can people be hurt if the media always says what it thinks?
- How does the law protect people?
- How can the media be influenced?
- Why is there a link between press freedom and democracy?

On one hand

If the media is not free:

- people do not know what is happening
- governments will decide what they want people to know
- it is hard for people to decide who to vote for if they haven't got enough information
- a country with limited press freedom is unlikely to be democratic.

On the other hand

The media can damage people's lives if it tells lies about them. The media can be influenced by:

- what the readers want to see
- advertisers
- its owners.

The media needs to be controlled by law to prevent these things happening.

Many people would think that both points of view have some value so this section shows how an A-grade candidate's answer makes this clear.

It is clear that countries which do not have freedom of the press are often not very democratic so there is a case for making sure that the press can tell us what is going on. In some countries, like Zimbabwe, the government doesn't want people to know how bad things are – and also threatens people who do not support them. In the UK we would not have known anything about MPs fiddling their expenses if the Daily Telegraph hadn't made headlines of it. They had to change the rules as a result.

While I agree that the press should be free I also agree that there are some things that it should not be doing. There are laws to protect people from discrimination so papers must not criticize them on grounds of sex, disability, age, race or religion. The laws about libel and slander also mean that the media must tell the truth or they can be sued. Newspapers can be very careful about what they say about people in case they are sued. For example, some papers told readers about Tiger Woods getting into trouble but others didn't take the risk.

I think we need a balance between the two. Press freedom is important to keep democracy going but it must be limited so people are not going to be hurt.

Knowing a country where press freedom is limited and its effect shows that you understand the relationship with democracy. The story about UK MPs' expenses has the same effect.

The student is saying that both points of view can be right – and supporting the argument.

Knowing how the law affects the issue always helps in this part of the course. You do not need to know the details of the law – but what they are about.

The final paragraph draws the discussion to a close and sums up the student's view that there is right on both sides.

2.2 How the media informs and influences public opinion

You will revise

- **The power of the media to influence public opinion**
- **The role of opinion polls • The role of pressure groups •**

Know the facts

In the exam you will be asked questions to test your knowledge of the key facts, so it is really important to learn them. Write a sentence for each of the key facts to show you understand what they mean. You will need to use an example in each sentence, so if you can't think of one – go and look it up!

Data Protection Act (DPA)	**opinion poll**	**stakeholder**
a UK law designed to protect personal information that is stored on computers or in an organised paper filing system	questioning a sample of the population to build a picture of the views of the public on a particular topic	someone who has an interest in a decision that is being made

Think about

What factors might have influenced the way people voted in this opinion poll?

The power of opinion polls

There are opinion polls in the newspapers every day. They are used as evidence by governments and pressure groups.

	Agree	Disagree	Don't know
The war in Afghanistan is unwinnable	63%	27%	10%
Corruption in the elections in Afghanistan show the war is not worth fighting	63%	31%	6%
British forces should be withdrawn from Afghanistan as soon as possible	52%	36%	12%

The power of pressure groups

Why does the media take up such campaigns? Can you think of a current issue that a newspaper or television programme has taken up?

Pressure groups usually campaign on one issue and seek to attract public attention for their cause.

The media sometimes take up an issue and campaign for it – with the aim of changing the law or the government's approach. Pressure groups will work to achieve this as it gives them a bigger voice.

One example of a campaign that the media has taken up in this way is 'Sarah's Law', which aims to help protect children. Another example is the campaign against fox hunting.

The role of government

The media might want to change government actions but the government also wants to influence the media. It wants people to believe in what it does and re-elect it at the next election – so it wants to look good.

Spin doctors are employed by political parties to make sure the media hears the right messages. People can be influenced by the information you give them. If the information is not accurate, the effect can be very damaging. If the media doesn't present a balanced view, it is difficult for people to make informed decisions.

Think about

Why is the government concerned about its public image?

In the exam

1 What is an opinion poll? *1 mark*

2 Which of the following pressure groups campaigns against the unfair treatment of prisoners?

   A Amnesty International

   B Shelter

   C Greenpeace

   D Unite *1 mark*

3 Explain why the government uses spin doctors to influence the media and the public. *2 marks*

Don't forget!

Questions are often asked about the difference between political parties and pressure groups.

Raising your grade

'The media should just tell us the news and not express opinions.'

Do you agree with this view?

Give reasons for your opinion, showing you have considered another point of view. You should support your argument with examples wherever possible.

- Why is it important for people to know what is in the news?
- How can people be affected if the news is biased?
- Is it possible to separate news and opinion?
- Do people need to be aware of different points of view?

On one hand

- People need to know the news in order to work out their own views.
- They need clear facts – not just someone's views.
- If the news is biased they will not be able to make unbiased decisions.
- In countries where the media is biased towards the government, democracy is often weak.

On the other hand

- It is difficult to explain the news without some bias.
- People can decide for themselves whether or not the news is biased.
- Some people wouldn't bother to read it at all if they did not agree with its point of view.
- It is good to see different opinions because it helps you to make up your mind.

Here is the second half of an A-grade answer.

This sentence builds on a bullet point and uses it to build an argument. The student doesn't just repeat it – she explains it and adds more information.

Most news has some bias because it is difficult to separate fact from opinion. People in other countries might say that the news in the UK is seen from a British point of view. The BBC and ITV have a duty to give an unbiased view but other news sources don't.

This shows that the student knows the background as well as having a point of view.

It is not always easy for people to see that the news is biased because they often read a paper that agrees with their own point of view. It is therefore important that they are given an unbiased view as well.

The student understands that it is hard to shift people's point of view, which can make it difficult to explain the facts.

The opening to the final paragraph explains the student's point of view clearly.

Although we need the news to be as unbiased as possible, it helps if people do see different opinions because they may develop a more balanced view. This is particularly important because it helps people to decide who they want to vote for in an election. This is good for democracy.

This piece of work also shows that you don't need to write at great length to get an A grade.

2.3 The justice system

You will revise

• Why we need laws • Civil and criminal law • How the law works •

Know the facts

In the exam you will be asked questions to test your knowledge of the key facts, so it is really important to learn them. Write a sentence for each of the key facts to show you understand what they mean. You will need to use an example in each sentence, so if you can't think of one – go and look it up!

civil law

this covers disputes between individuals or groups. Civil law cases are often about rights

county court

a local court that has limited powers in civil cases

criminal law

this deals with offences such as murder and drug dealing. These cases are between the Crown Prosecution Service (acting for all citizens) and the offender

crown court

courts held in towns in England and Wales where judges hear cases

High Court

the court where judges hear cases on serious crimes

magistrates' court

a court held before two or more public officers dealing with minor crimes

small claims court

a local court, which hears civil cases involving small amounts of money

judge

a person who decides questions of law in a court

judiciary

all the judges in a country

barrister

a lawyer who represents and speaks for their clients in court

jury

a group of people who decide if someone is guilty in a court of law

probation officer

someone who writes court reports on offenders and supervises them in the community

solicitor

a lawyer who gives legal advice and may speak for their clients in court

recorder

a barrister or solicitor of at least ten years' experience, who acts as a part-time judge in a crown court

sue

to make a claim against someone or something

mitigating

making something less intense or severe

What are the issues?

Think about

Are there other reasons why we need laws? Why do most people obey the law?

Why do we need laws?

Is it dishonest to ….

1 take stationery home from work?

2 connect to a neighbour's WiFi without permission?

3 copy another student's coursework from the internet?

4 make an insurance claim and include damage that had happened before?

Below are the results of asking a group of males and females the above questions. They seem to show that males and females tend to think differently about dishonesty.

	Males answering 'Yes'	Females answering 'Yes'
Question 1	78%	85%
Question 2	79%	85%
Question 3	79%	88%
Question 4	85%	92%

Source: Adapted from www.honestylab.com

What is the difference between civil and criminal law?

What sort of law would deal with the story behind the headline? Think of some recent examples of both types of law.

Civil law is about disputes between individuals or groups. The arguments are often about rights. Examples include company law, adoption, accidents at work and consumer rights.

Criminal law deals with offences such as murder, theft and drug dealing. In a criminal case, the conflict is between the government and the lawbreakers.

Man shot over dispute about hedge

Who is involved in the law?

Who are the people in the picture?

What role does each of the people listed play in the legal system?

Many people are involved in the justice system.

- Judges
- Magistrates
- Jury
- Police
- Solicitors
- Barristers
- Probation officers.

What is the role of juries?

For	Against
Trials are held in public.	Juries are sometimes wrong.
A jury's decision is not political.	Juries are often not the same mix of people as the rest of society.
People should have the right to be involved in the legal system.	Juries cost at least £120 million each year.
People are more likely to vote if they have been on a jury.	Cases can be complex.

Think about

Some politicians would like to get rid of juries. What do you think would happen if there were no juries?

What is the difference between a crown court and magistrates' court?

Over 95 per cent of all criminal trials take place in magistrates' courts. Specially trained magistrates also run youth courts for offenders aged between 10 and 17.

The most serious criminal cases are heard in a crown court. The judges and barristers wear wigs and gowns. A jury decides if the defendant is guilty or not.

- High Court judges, who sit in the larger courts, can try very serious cases, such as murder and rape.

- Circuit judges and recorders try less serious cases such as theft.

What are the main differences between the two types of court?

What sort of penalties can courts impose?

A magistrate can impose:

- prison sentences up to a maximum of six months
- community sentences
- Antisocial Behaviour Orders (ASBOs)
- fines up to a maximum of £5000
- Discharges – conditional or absolute.

A crown court can impose penalties up to life imprisonment.

Why do you think crown courts can impose more serious penalties?

'I made a genuine mistake on the A3 heading into London. It was dark and I didn't see the sign showing the speed change from 70 to 50, and got caught by the camera doing 77 mph. It was the first time I had used this bit of road in the dark and I didn't notice the signs because none of them are illuminated.'

Weigh up whether you think the driver's mitigating circumstances were strong enough to be let off – or get a reduced penalty?

In the exam

1 What is a jury?   *1 mark*

2 What is the difference between a barrister and a solicitor?   *1 mark*

3 Which of the following statements about a crown court is true?

   A A crown court can impose unlimited prison sentences.

   B In a crown court a person's guilt or innocence is decided by a jury.

   C A magistrate sits in a crown court.

   D Mitigating factors are not taken into account.   *1 mark*

Raising your grade

'Everyone should always obey the law.'

Do you agree with this view?

Give reasons for your opinion, showing you have considered another point of view. You should support your argument with examples wherever possible.

- Is the law always right – or can people who disagree with it break it?
- Can you break the speed limit, or steal, in an emergency?
- If we don't like a law, should we protest peacefully, rather than just breaking the law?
- If we want to live in a law-abiding society should we all keep the law?

On one hand

- Laws are made to protect people.
- They are in the interest of most people.
- There would be chaos if we could pick and choose.
- Laws were made democratically, so we should obey them.

On the other hand

- There may be mitigating circumstances.
- Protest may be the only way to try to change the law, but protesting may be against the law.
- Society sometimes changes faster than the law does.
- Governments may want to control what we can do.

Here's the introduction from an A-grade candidate.

We live in a democratic country and laws are made democratically, so we should usually obey them. There may be circumstances when it may be difficult to do so – or when we don't want to.

> The student sets out more than one point of view straight away – so already has achieved at least a C grade.

Although laws are made democratically, they don't always meet everyone's needs. The suffragettes had to break the law in order to get votes for women. We have had to introduce laws to protect people from all sorts of discrimination. Gay people used to break the law until it was changed. Now things have moved on and they are also protected from discrimination. Society often changes before the law catches up.

> The reference to suffragettes shows that the student is making links between difference sections of the specification.

People argue that the government has been limiting our human rights by keeping DNA samples on record. It is possible to protest against laws like this without breaking the law. A case has been taken to the European Court of Human Rights about this – and they won – so the UK has to change its rules.

> This is an up-to-date example of how people can change the law. It again connects different parts of the specification to build an argument.

When the government doesn't want us to protest about an issue, it may try to make protest illegal. You can now only have small protests outside Parliament, so they are not so effective. People who want their voices to be heard might want to break this law. I think if you really care about something you should be allowed to protest.

> The last sentence shows that the student has a strong point of view. It would be even better if they thought about how breaking the law might affect people.

2.4 The voice of democracy

You will revise

- **What is meant by representative democracy**
- **The organisation and work of the local council** • **What pressure groups do** •

Know the facts

In the exam you will be asked questions to test your knowledge of the key facts so it is really important to learn them! Write a sentence including each key fact to show you understand what it means. You will need to use an example in the sentence so if you can't think of one – go and look it up!

representative democracy

a type of democracy where citizens have the right to choose someone to represent them on a council or in Parliament as an MP

school council

a group of people who represent the classes and year groups of the school. They give students the opportunity to participate in decision-making

council

a group of people who are elected to look after the affairs of a town, district or county

councillor

a member of a local council, elected by people in that area

manifesto

a published statement of the aims and policies of a political party

political party

an organised group of people with common aims who put up candidates for elections

polling station

a place where votes are cast; often a school, library or village hall

ward

an area that forms a separate part of a local council

business rates

a form of tax paid by all the businesses in an area. The amount a business pays depends on the rent that could be charged for their premises

council tax

a tax paid by everyone who lives in an area. It is based on the value of their house

Forward Plan

a document that sets out the aims of the council in the long term

minutes

a formal record of what has been said at a meeting

ombudsman

a person who investigates complaints against the government or a public organisation

youth council

a group of young people who meet to discuss what is going on in the local area and put their ideas to the council

Think about

How do school councils help young people to understand how democracy works?

How are representatives chosen?

Why have a school council?
- to increase awareness of the democratic process
- to express views about matters that concern students in school
- to have an input into the school's decisions
- to ensure that your views are heard and valued.

The election

On the afternoon of the election, students are called into the hall year by year where they are given a ballot paper with the names of the nominees from their year. They choose two of the nominees from each class to represent them and then place their ballot paper into the ballot box. The results of the election are normally announced the next day in the school's assembly.

How are councillors chosen?

Why are most councils a mix of different parties? Why is it important for the ballot to be secret?

The local council is made up of local people who make decisions about local services. These councillors represent different parts of the town, called wards. The people who live in the ward choose councillors in an election.

Political parties put forward candidates for people to choose. Each party will have already decided on a list of plans, called a manifesto. The plans will be put into practice if the party wins enough seats on the council.

The list of people comes from the well-known political parties such as Labour, Conservatives and Liberal Democrats, as well as smaller groups like the Green Party. People who are independent or are campaigning on a local issue stand for election too. Most councils are a mix of political parties, but the party with most councillors takes overall control.

You vote at a polling station – and it is secret, so nobody can check on your decision.

What sorts of decisions are made locally?

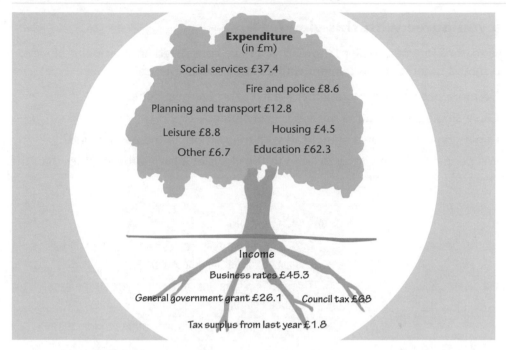

Expenditure
(in £m)

Social services £37.4

Fire and police £8.6

Planning and transport £12.8

Leisure £8.8   Housing £4.5

Other £6.7   Education £62.3

Income

Business rates £45.3

General government grant £26.1   Council tax £68

Tax surplus from last year £1.8

How can you influence the local council?

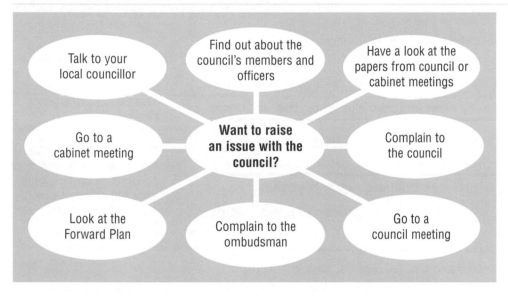

Talk to your local councillor

Find out about the council's members and officers

Have a look at the papers from council or cabinet meetings

Go to a cabinet meeting

Want to raise an issue with the council?

Complain to the council

Look at the Forward Plan

Complain to the ombudsman

Go to a council meeting

How can pressure groups influence the council?

Some friends really wanted a BMX track. They formed a group to put a plan together. They went to the council who accepted their plan – if they could raise half the money for it. They organized all sorts of fundraising and the track was built.

In the exam

1 What is the difference between a political party and a pressure group?   *2 marks*

2 What is representative democracy?   *1 mark*

3 Give two benefits of having a youth council in your local area.   *2 marks*

Raising your grade

'A pressure group is usually more effective than individuals working alone.'

Do you agree with this view?

Give reasons for your opinion, showing you have considered another point of view. You should support your argument with examples wherever possible.

- Do more people working together mean that more gets done?
- Can a single person with a mission be very effective?
- Can a single person be a figurehead with many more in the background?
- Will people be more willing to listen to the views of a large group, rather than the views of just one person?

On one hand

- A group of people is more representative of the views of the community.
- A group will have more skills to build a campaign.
- A group will have more time to spend on the campaign.
- The organization to be influenced will have to listen if many people contact them.

On the other hand

- One person who really cares about something can be successful in persuading others.
- There will only be one view to present so the case could be clearer.
- In the end, they may persuade others to join them.

Here's an A-grade answer that demonstrates the use of the bullets.

A group of people is generally more effective than an individual. The bullet points show that there are, however, two sides to the argument.

The first point says that more gets done if more people are involved. This is usually true because they will have more time between them. Everyone needs to be committed. It can be hard work organising people if they are not – and this can take more time than just doing it yourself.

A single person who really wants to have an effect can do a lot – and they don't have to worry about the views of others. If they do get their voice heard, others may join them. This means that they will be the figurehead, but have plenty of help as the campaign grows.

The final bullet point says that a group will be more effective because the council, for example, will be more likely to listen if there are more people. This is probably true because the council is democratic and the councillors will probably want to get re-elected so they should listen to what the voters want.

Although there are two sides to the argument, I believe that ...

This shows that the student recognises that the bullets give them the basis for arguing from both sides.

The student has recognised that the bullet point is there for discussion. It can be used to argue both points of view.

This point does the same.

The student looks at the longer-term effects. Campaigns do not stand still and others might join in.

2.5 The role of democracy

You will revise

- **How MPs are elected and what they do** • **How laws are made**
- **How government is influenced by public opinion** •

Know the facts

In the exam you will be asked questions to test your knowledge of the key facts, so it is really important to learn them. Write a sentence for each of the key facts to show you understand what they mean. You will need to use an example in each sentence, so if you can't think of one – go and look it up!

canvassing

when people try to persuade others to vote for their party in an election

Member of Parliament

a person who has been elected to represent a constituency in Parliament

Speaker

the MP elected to act as chairman for debates in the House of Commons

lobby

to try to persuade MPs to support a particular point of view. This used to happen in the 'lobby', or hallway, on the way into Parliament

Cabinet

group of MPs who head major government departments. Meets weekly to make decisions about how government policy will be carried out

House of Commons

the more powerful of the two parts of the British Parliament. Its members are elected by the public

Prime Minister

the leader of the majority party in the House of Commons and the leader of the government

Secretary of State

an MP who is in charge of a government department such as health or defence

Minister of State

an assistant to the Secretary of State

Shadow Cabinet

MPs from the main opposition party who 'shadow' MPs who head major government departments

accountable

if you are accountable for something, you are responsible for it and have to explain your actions

public consultation

involves asking the public about their opinions on changes in the law, policies or large-scale developments

Green Paper

puts forward ideas that the government wants discussed before it starts to develop policy

White Paper

puts government policy up for discussion before it becomes law

Opposition

political parties who are not in power

constituency

the area represented by an MP

public opinion

the popular view

Act

law passed by parliament

bill

proposal to change something into law

general election

an election for a new government – at least every five years in the UK

advocacy

arguing on behalf of a particular issue

Why do you think people want to become MPs?

How do you become an MP?

Jo Swinson was the youngest MP when she was first elected to the House of Commons

Getting elected

Most MPs are selected by one of the political parties to be its candidate at an election. They are chosen to represent a constituency. If they win the election, they then become the MP who represents everyone in the area.

A few people stand as independents and therefore do not go through the party system. For example, Doctor Richard Taylor was furious that the local hospital was to be closed. He stood as an independent and won the seat.

Who shall I vote for?

How and why do these factors influence your decision about who to vote for?

All sorts of things affect people's decision about how to cast their vote.

- What is your age, gender or ethnicity?
- What social class are you in?
- Where do you live?
- What do your friends think?
- What is your religion?
- Which papers do you read?
- What do you think of the parties' policies?

What do MPs do?

What do the people do who are shown in the picture of the House of Commons?

1 Speaker
2 Prime Minister
3 Cabinet
4 Secretaries of State
5 Opposition
6 Shadow Cabinet
7 Backbenchers

How are laws made?

First reading
A bill is introduced in the House of Commons. Before it reaches this stage, it has been worked on by a Drafting Committee to make sure that it is correctly put together.

Second reading
The bill is debated fully in the House of Commons. A vote is taken and if the majority of MPs approve of the bill, it is passed.

Standing committee
A group of MPs look at the bill carefully and make any alterations that are needed.

Report stage
The committee sends a report to the House of Commons with all its amendments. These amendments are either approved or changed.

Royal assent
Once the bill has passed all its stages in the Commons and the Lords, it is sent to the Queen for her signature. This is really a formality, as the Queen would never refuse to sign a bill that had been through the democratic process. The bill then becomes an Act of Parliament and part of the law of the country.

House of Lords
The bill goes through the same process as in the Commons. If the Lords want to change anything, the bill is returned to the Commons.

Third reading
The bill is presented to the House of Commons. It is debated and a vote is taken.

Think about
What is the difference between a bill and an Act? Why do you think there are so many stages in making a law?

Don't forget!
- **Parliament** is made up of all the MPs who are elected, plus members of the House of Lords. The **government** is made up of MPs belonging to the party that holds power in parliament.

Pressure groups or political parties?

Pressure groups often work to promote a cause such as looking after the environment, like the World Wide Fund for Nature and Friends of the Earth, or by helping relieve housing problems, like Shelter. Trade unions and other organisations are pressure groups that work to protect the interests of their members.

A **political party** is an organised group of people with common aims who put up candidates for elections. They have policies that deal with all aspects of running the country from the economy to health, education, transport, etc.

Why would you join either a political party or a pressure group? Why are both important?

The influence of voluntary organizations

Voluntary organizations aim to look after people and have a mission. They try to persuade the government to make changes that will improve life for the people they work with. They also want to influence public opinion in order to encourage the government to listen.

How can voluntary organisations influence government?

Consulting the public?

The government also carries out consultations to ask the public what they think. If you Google 'government consultations' you can see long lists of consultations that are currently being carried out. They cover a range of issues, for example rules about dangerous dogs, ways of choosing a GP, or strategies to prevent violence against women. They often offer the government's plans and ask for people's views on what should happen.

How does consultation help the government to make policy? Why do you think it consults the public?

Don't forget!
- Vountary organisations are bodies whose activities are carried out for reasons other than profit, but do not inclue any public or local authority.

In the exam

1 What is a constituency? *1 mark*

2 What is the difference between an MP and a Secretary of State? *2 marks*

3 What is the difference between a Bill and an Act? *2 marks*

Exam tip

Even if you have strong views on an issue, it is important to remember to put another point of view – and support it. Don't exaggerate!

Raising your grade

'Too many MPs are too old. They cannot represent younger voters so many don't bother to vote.'

Do you agree with this view?

Give reasons for your opinion, showing you have considered another point of view. You should support your argument with examples wherever possible.

- Should MPs represent the age structure of the population?
- If they were younger, would they understand the needs of young people better?
- Would more young people vote if MPs were younger?
- Does the age of MPs matter?

On one hand

- The average age of MPs is very high.
- They talk a different language from young people.
- Their work seems to have nothing to do with us.
- I would vote if I thought they would listen to my point of view – but they are all too old.

On the other hand

- MPs have had a lot of experience of life and should be able to make better decisions.
- We have an ageing population, so there should be more MPs who are older.

Here's part of an answer from an A-grade student who has very strong views.

> This student has strong opinions – and they have exaggerated their case. Not all MPs are very old. It is important to be accurate in your claims.

MPs are all very old. When you see them on the telly they don't seem to talk the same language as me and my friends. It is a pity because it makes us less interested in what they have to say. Even when it is very important, it does not seem to relate to us. People complain that young people aren't interested but MPs don't make much effort to include us in what they have to say. I always turn over when party political broadcasts come on because they are always stuffy. We hear a lot about how the parties have spin doctors to give the public a good impression of what they do – but they never seem to remember people like me.

> Party political broadcasts are used to communicate with the voters, so the student is using knowledge well to support their argument.

> Despite the strong views, the student puts another point of view and explains it well by pointing out that other voters might want someone older.

I do understand that other people have different views and that it might be difficult to get elected if you are very young. The voters might think that you have not had enough experience of life if you are young. We have an ageing population, so there is a case for having older MPs as well as younger ones – but they should learn to communicate with people of all ages.

> Knowing that we have an ageing population adds useful information to support another point of view.

2.6 Does democracy work?

You will revise

- **The changing nature of democracy in the UK** • **New ways of voting**
- **Different ways of running a country** •

Know the facts

In the exam you will be asked questions to test your knowledge of the key facts, so it is really important to learn them. Write a sentence for each of the key facts to show you understand what they mean. You will need to use an example in each sentence, so if you can't think of one – go and look it up!

Assembly

a body of people elected to decide on some areas of spending in a region

devolution

the transfer of power from central to regional government

hereditary peers

people who inherited the title 'Lord' or 'Lady'

people's peers

people who are selected to sit in the House of Lords

referendum

a vote by the whole electorate on a particular issue

electorate

all those registered to vote

first past the post

an electoral system where voters have one vote per constituency and the candidate with the most votes wins

postal vote

when voters make their vote by post, rather than by going to a polling station

proportional representation

an electoral system in which the number of seats a party wins is roughly proportional to its national share of the vote

dictatorship

a country's leader makes all the decisions with no reference to the population

Why do referenda and devolution make the UK more democratic?

Why does having hereditary peers in the House of Lords and fewer people voting make the UK less democratic? Why can it be difficult to change things?

Could the UK be more democratic?

More democratic	*Less democratic*
Referendum	Unelected House of Lords
Devolution	Fall in the number of people voting

A Swiss referendum votes to ban minarets on mosques.

The North East votes against regional government.

Persuading people to vote

'**First past the post**' is the system used for general elections in the UK. People have one vote in one constituency and the candidate with the most votes becomes the MP for that area. If you added all the votes in the country together, sometimes the winning party does not have the most votes.

Proportional representation, or PR, means that every vote counts. The constituencies are larger, so each one elects five or six people. Voters put all the candidates in order of preference, putting 1 against their favourite candidate, 2 against their second favourite, and so on. Candidates with the most votes overall win their seats in government.

Democracy or dictatorship?

Think about

If a county has elections, how can it not be democratic?

President Mugabe has warned Zimbabwe that he expects elections soon, raising fears among the Opposition that he will again mount a campaign of terror and violence to stay in power.

In the exam

1 What is the electorate?   *1 mark*

2 Which voting method is used in a British general election?

   A Hereditary

   B Proportional representation

   C First past the post

   D Referendum   *1 mark*

3 a What is a dictatorship?

   b Name one disadvantage of a dictatorship   *2 marks*

Don't forget!

First past the post helps the main parties – so they like it. PR would give the Liberal Democrats and the Greens more seats.

Exam tip

If you can see good reasons for both sides of the argument, debate the two but make sure you come to a conclusion – even if you want to explain your reservations.

Raising your grade

'Devolution gives better government because it is local government.'

Do you agree with this view?

Give reasons for your opinion, showing you have considered another point of view. You should support your argument with examples wherever possible.

- Do local people know what their area really needs?
- Is regional government worth the extra cost?
- Are there issues that need different solutions in different parts of the country?
- Should we be more European and encourage decisions to be made by European government?

On one hand

- The regions are very different in some ways and should have different laws.
- Regional government is expensive but it is worth it to get the right decision.
- You could remove a level of local government to pay for it.
- Europe is too big and too different to make laws for our regions.

On the other hand

- The UK cannot afford to have more layers of government.
- The UK is too small to have different laws in different places.
- People in the North East rejected a regional assembly, so would the others?
- If you have different taxes in different parts of the country, people will move to where the taxes are lower.

Here is an answer from an A-grade student who doesn't have a strong point of view but comes up with a sensible argument.

There are arguments for and against this statement. Devolution means giving power to regional government. Whether it works probably depends on the powers that are to be handed over. It would be difficult to have different policies on things like defence and trade but there are some that could be more local. Local decisions are already made about health and education but central government has overall control of them. Some people argue that it would be better to be really local. Others say that central government control helps to keep standards up.

> The introduction shows that the student is going to weigh up the arguments.

> The rest of the writing shows how the student looks at both sides of the argument. The notes the student has written on the hands shows the two sides very clearly. They are then used very effectively.

> Here there are comparisons using real examples to show both sides of the argument.

At this point the student continues the argument before coming to a conclusion ...

There are good arguments on both sides but I think that devolution is the right thing to do because it is important to make good decisions for different areas. I would, however, look very carefully at the powers that are devolved. This might depend on how much the people want it. Scotland has more powers than Wales, partly because more people were in favour of devolution when they voted in the referendum in Scotland.

> The conclusion is important – especially when you are unsure which side you really agree with. Here the student comes to a conclusion but gives it conditions.

> Dropping in some knowledge from the 'facts' help to convince the examiner that you really know your stuff!

3.1 Achieving sustainability

You will revise

- **The meaning of sustainable development**
- **Ways in which Local Agenda 21 can support sustainability**
- **International efforts to support sustainability •**

Know the facts

In the exam you will be asked questions to test your knowledge of the key facts, so it is really important to learn them. Write a sentence for each of the key facts to show you understand what they mean. You will need to use an example in each sentence, so if you can't think of one – go and look it up!

renewable	**sustainable development**	**Local Agenda 21**
able to be replaced or restored	living now in a way that doesn't damage the needs of future generations	a global plan to ask local people how they think their immediate environment could be improved

What is sustainable development? Think of an example to show you understand each part of the diagram.

What is sustainability?

promotes local solutions to problems

values all people and species

promotes the planet's water, air and soil

Sustainable development

promotes and protects diversity

protects the needs of future generations

Can LA21 help?

Why is LA21 about more than the environment? Think of some examples of LA21 projects.

Local Agenda 21 is a 'global' plan but it stresses the importance of involving local people when planning projects. It is about more than the environment. It involves education, employment and people working in their community in all sorts of ways. Local people often have valuable knowledge and experience, and are more likely to support a project if they feel they 'own' it. All LA21 projects should provide for the needs of the local community as a whole, and not exclude or discriminate against any group or minority.

What's happening in Europe?

Why do you think that some EU countries are unhappy about the burden of cuts?

Some countries have threatened to block a deal for EU-wide cuts in greenhouse gas emissions. Some Eastern and central European countries are unhappy at the burden of cuts they will be expected to bear under the existing climate agreement.

What is the UN trying to achieve?

```
                    UN's Millennium Goals

  prevent extreme        achieve universal      promote gender
  poverty and hunger     primary education      equality and
                                                empower women

  reduce                 UN's                   improve
  child mortality        Millennium             maternal wealth
                         Goals

  combat HIV/AIDS,       ensure environmental   develop a global
  malaria and            sustainability         partnership for
  other diseases                                development
```

Think about

How do you think each of the Millennium Goals will contribute to sustainability?

In the exam

1 Give two reasons why the UK is not sustainable.   *2 marks*

2 Name two renewable sources of energy.   *2 marks*

3 Explain how Local Agenda 21 can help to achieve sustainability.   *2 marks*

Don't forget!

Sustainability is not just about the environment – but all the activities that help make communities work – such as employment, education and decent housing.

Raising your grade

'Rich countries should help poor countries to cut their emissions of carbon dioxide.'

Do you agree with this view?

Give reasons for your opinion, showing you have considered another point of view. You should support your argument with examples wherever possible.

- Did rich countries cause the problem because they developed earlier?
- Is it fair that poor countries should have their development held back by limits on their production of greenhouse gases?
- Why should rich countries have to pay to help poor countries?
- Should rich countries help China and India, which are developing fast?

On one hand

- We must stop global warming, so countries must work together.
- People in rich countries have lots of advantages. They should give something up to stop global warming.
- There are lots of people in poor countries who are very poor though some are getting rich.
- Helping poor countries will make the world fairer.

On the other hand

- China and India are growing very quickly, so do they really need help?
- If richer countries help poorer ones, they could be helping them sell things that they themselves could sell.
- It has been suggested that targets should be set for poor countries but they should be given time to get there.

Here is an answer from an A-grade student.

We must all work together to solve global warming because of the effect it will have on our way of life. We will not be able to grow the crops we grow now and lots of the world will become desert if we don't solve the problem.

Very poor countries have small carbon footprints because they use very little energy – but they do cut down trees for firewood. We certainly need to help them to develop because it helps to make the world fairer. They will then be able to grow in a way that does not damage the environment.

International agreements are difficult to make because everyone has their own interests – as we saw in the 2009 conference in Copenhagen. Some rich countries don't want to give anything up and some LEDCs want to be free to develop new industries without worrying about the environment.

While I think we need to help the poorest countries, the middling countries like China and India are growing very fast and they must join in and accept some responsibility themselves.

We do need to find a way of agreeing. People need to compromise if we are to make an agreement that sticks.

The student is showing an understanding of the differences between countries.

Here is the start of an ethical view. Asking how you can make things better without harming others would develop this idea.

The mention of the Copenhagen summit on climate change shows knowledge of relevant world events.

This shows a balanced and reasoned discussion based on good knowledge.

3.2 The economy at work

You will revise

- **How the economy works** • **The effect of inflation**
- **The effect of borrowing** • **Balancing the budget**•

Know the facts

In the exam you will be asked questions to test your knowledge of the key facts, so it is really important to learn them. Write a sentence for each of the key facts to show you understand what they mean. You will need to use an example in each sentence, so if you can't think of one – go and look it up!

the economy all the organisations that provide goods and services, and all the individuals and organisations that buy them	**private sector** section of the economy made up of businesses or organisations that are owned by individuals or by shareholders	**public sector** section of the economy made up of organisations owned or run by the government and local councils
profit money you gain when you sell something for more than you paid for it or than it cost to make	**shareholder** someone who owns part of a business by owning shares in a company	**division of labour** where employees concentrate on a particular task or job at which they are expert
interdependent where businesses need each other to survive	**specialised** where employees or businesses concentrate on tasks that they can do well	**retraining** learning new skills that can be used in a different job
inflation the general rise in prices	**deflation** the general fall in prices	**rate of inflation** the rate at which prices rise
economic growth when the country is producing more goods and services than the year before	**interest** extra payment made to a lender by a borrower	**poverty line** the income level below which someone cannot afford to live
redistributing income taking money from wealthier people through taxation, to give it to poorer people through benefits	**Chancellor of the Exchequer** the member of the government who is responsible for the country's finances	**the Budget** the process each year when the Chancellor of the Exchequer explains how the government will raise and spend its money
government revenue the money raised by the government		

What do the people shown here have in common? Use the pictures to think about how an economy works.

What is an economy?

Why are we all interdependent?

How are you dependent on other people in your local area? How are you dependent on people further away?

A long time ago, people in Britain were mostly self-sufficient. They built their houses, grew their food and made their clothes. Today we specialise, so we earn money doing what we are best at and buy things from other people. This is known as division of labour. It is more efficient because we are using our skills to best effect.

We are also dependent on people in other countries. For example, we buy oranges, cocoa and many other things from round the world. We can't grow some things and other countries make lots of things more cheaply than we can in Britain.

Is it fair?

Why do you think competition works well? Why do you think the person in the picture has lost out?

Competition drives the economy. People who do things best get jobs. Businesses do well if they sell products that people want at prices they are happy to pay. This means that some people and businesses lose out.

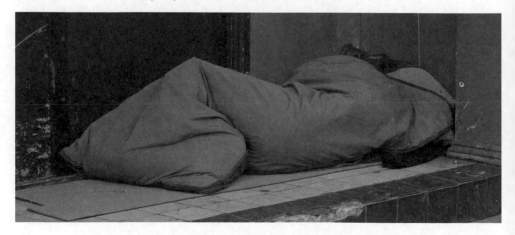

What is inflation?

Think about

Is it better to be a saver or a borrower when there is inflation? Who loses out when prices rise?

How does the government try to control inflation?

Borrowing: good or bad?

People use the money they earn each month to buy products and services. If they have some money left when they have bought everything they need, they can save.

If you want to borrow money, you must find someone to lend it. You will pay interest on the loan. This is an amount of money paid in addition to the amount borrowed so everything you buy on credit will cost more in the end. It is only safe to borrow money if you know you can pay it back.

What do you borrow and save for? Why can it be risky to borrow? What sort of things do families borrow money to buy?

Taxing or spending

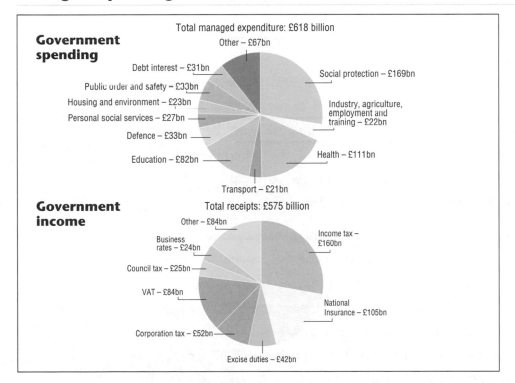

If the government decides it wants to spend more on education, what choices does it have?

How do you think government spending might influence the way people vote?

In the exam

1 What is inflation? *1 mark*

2 Explain why government spending might influence how people vote. *2 marks*

3 Why does the government run schemes to retrain people in new skills? *2 marks*

Don't forget!

If the government wants to spend more it must either raise taxes or borrow more money, so it's not easy to make changes by spending more.

Exam tip

If you have a strong point of view on an issue, you must make sure that you really show that there is another point of view. You may want to show why you think it is wrong but you still need to set out the argument.

'If the National Health Service needs more money, it should have it.'

Do you agree with this view?

Give reasons for your opinion, showing you have considered another point of view. You should support your argument with examples wherever possible.

On one hand

- If people need health care they should have it.
- If there is not enough money the NHS has to decide which people will be treated.
- Taxes should be increased to pay for it.

On the other hand

- If the NHS gets all the money it wants, other government spending will have to be reduced.
- The NHS could be more efficient.
- If taxes are increased people might not vote for the party at the next election.

This shows how an A-grade student who has strong opinions makes sure that he puts both sides of the argument.

This shows that the student understands that there are trade-offs in the decisions that governments have to make on spending.

Current evidence is used and developed to show both sides of the argument.

The student shows that he has a good knowledge of how government spending works.

The final sentence shows that the student understands the links to the reasons why political decisions are made.

The NHS needs to be well funded. People's health is important but it may not be possible to provide all the money that is needed for everything.

Governments do not have unlimited amounts of money to spend. They have to raise money from taxes, so how much they spend will affect the amount of tax we pay. While it is important that health, education and all the other services that the government provides are paid for, the party in power can decide how much to spend on each part.

There have been cases in the news where people have not been allowed to have a drug that would help them. It is very difficult to keep costs down without having rules but they are not always right. Campaigns have had some of these rulings overturned but this means that other people will not have treatment as there is a limit on the total amount of money. Perhaps the NHS could be more efficient so it could save money and have more to treat people.

I really want people to be treated but I also think education and other services are important too. Political parties do not want to lose elections, so they want to keep taxes down, as many people don't like paying taxes.

3.3 People's impact on the community

You will revise

- **How people and organizations can make a difference locally**
- **How people and organizations can make a difference globally** •

Know the facts

In the exam you will be asked questions to test your knowledge of the key facts, so it is really important to learn them. Write a sentence for each of the key facts to show you understand what they mean. You will need to use an example in each sentence, so if you can't think of one – go and look it up!

volunteer	**voluntary organizations**	**refugee**
someone who works for free for a community	organisations with a social purpose that do not aim to make a profit	person who has been forced to leave their country and must live somewhere else

Think about

Do people volunteer just to help others? What other reasons do they have?

Why volunteer?

	% of respondents
I wanted to improve things, help people	53
Cause was important to me	41
I had time to spare	41
I wanted to meet people	30
Connected with needs, interests of family or friends	29
There was a need in the community	29
Friends/family did it	21
To learn new skills	19
Part of my religious belief	17
To help get on in my career	7
Had received voluntary help myself	4
Already involved in the organisation	2
Connected with my interests, hobbies	2
To give something back	1

Source: www.cabinetoffice.gov.uk

Why do businesses get involved in volunteering?

Why do you think some businesses encourage their staff to volunteer?

The picture shows people who work for Costain, the construction company, painting murals on the walls in a primary school playground.

How do voluntary organizations bring about change?

Amnesty International uses the power of the individual to put on the pressure. The organization publicises human rights abuses and asks its members to write to the relevant governments or authorities in protest. One letter would have little effect but hundreds or thousands might make people listen. These are the sorts of strategies used by many large pressure groups.

Who benefits?

Think about

How do other voluntary organizations persuade people and governments to change?

How would the UK be worse off if people did not do voluntary work?

Valuable helping hands in Leeds

In Leeds, volunteers carry out a wide range of work to help others across the city. They look after gardens, prepare people for the world of work, support older and disabled people in their homes and even run railways.

There is an army of nearly 20,000 unpaid volunteers who give up their time to help others. It is estimated that these voluntary organizations spend £45 million in the city. If the work of volunteers had to be paid for, it would cost about £40 million.

Source: Ripple Effect II, Leeds Voice

In the exam

1 What is a voluntary organization?   *1 mark*

2 Name two ways in which volunteers benefit from volunteering.   *2 marks*

Exam tip

Make sure that you finish well. Pick up the ideas that you have used in your writing and use them as evidence to give a strong conclusion.

Raising your grade

'The government should provide whatever people need. Voluntary organizations should not be necessary.'

Do you agree with this view?

Give reasons for your opinion, showing you have considered another point of view. You should support your argument with examples wherever possible.

On one hand

- We pay taxes, which should be enough to cover the services we expect the government to provide.
- Voluntary organizations depend on people's goodwill, which we cannot always depend on.
- Some voluntary organizations are more powerful than others because people support issues they are interested in. This may mean that some interests are ignored.

On the other hand

- If people are interested in particular issues, they should be encouraged to support them.
- The amount of government money is limited, so it can't support everything.
- Volunteers and those they support benefit from the work of these organizations.

This is a good ending to an answer. It shows how an A-grade student comes to a clear conclusion.

At the start of the conclusion, the student sets out her point of view with some explanation.

It is helpful to show the impact on the community, as this is the core of Citizenship.

The final sentence is a good round up of the student's point of view.

In conclusion, I do not agree with the statement that the government should provide everything that we might need. While it would be a good thing, the government does not have the money to do it unless it raises taxes to a high level.

I do support the view that voluntary organizations should be encouraged. Many people get a lot of satisfaction from working with voluntary organizations and often people who receive their services enjoy the company and care that is given. This can range from visiting old people to helping with the Guides and Scouts. Without these activities, communities would not be so strong.

The work of some of these organizations cannot be carried out by government in the same way. Members of Amnesty write letters to ask for freedom for prisoners in countries that do not respect human rights. It may not be possible, for political reasons, for the government to say what it thinks.

There are all sorts of voluntary organizations and I believe that they should be encouraged to express views and take action in the community.

This shows some strong evidence to support the conclusion.

This statement shows that the student has an understanding of the world context – which helps to support the argument.

3.4 The UK's role in the world

You will revise

- **The work of the European Union** • **The Commonwealth**
- **The United Nations and its work** •

Know the facts

In the exam you will be asked questions to test your knowledge of the key facts, so it is really important to learn them. Write a sentence for each of the key facts to show you understand what they mean. You will need to use an example in each sentence, so if you can't think of one – go and look it up!

Euro	**single currency**	**member state**
the name of the single currency used by a group of countries within the European Union	this is the Euro, so called as it is used in some of the EU member states	a country that is a member of the EU

European ombudsman	**Commonwealth of Nations**	**United Nations**
a person who investigates complaints against the EU	a voluntary group of independent countries	an international organization that tries to encourage peace, cooperation and friendship between countries

customs duty
taxes on products bought from other countries

What are the issues?

Think about

The EU member countries trade with each other. There are many rules about people's working conditions, product standards and the environment. Why do you think they are necessary?

What is the European Union?

The EU is a group of countries that aims to:

- promote economic and social progress
- give the EU a voice on the international scene
- introduce EU citizenship
- develop an area of freedom, security and justice
- maintain and establish EU regulations.

In early 2010 there were 29 member countries. Others are in the process of joining.

What does the EU do?

Which is the most powerful organization within the EU?

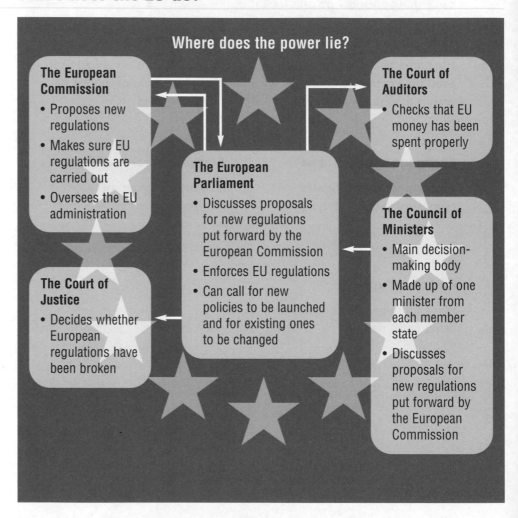

Where does the power lie?

The European Commission
- Proposes new regulations
- Makes sure EU regulations are carried out
- Oversees the EU administration

The Court of Auditors
- Checks that EU money has been spent properly

The European Parliament
- Discusses proposals for new regulations put forward by the European Commission
- Enforces EU regulations
- Can call for new policies to be launched and for existing ones to be changed

The Council of Ministers
- Main decision-making body
- Made up of one minister from each member state
- Discusses proposals for new regulations put forward by the European Commission

The Court of Justice
- Decides whether European regulations have been broken

How does the Commonwealth work?

Countries want to join the Commonwealth. Why do you think this is?

The Commonwealth of Nations is usually just called the Commonwealth. It is an association of countries, most of which were once ruled by Britain. However, today's Commonwealth is a world away from the handful of countries that were the first members. From Africa and Asia to the Pacific and the Caribbean, the Commonwealth's 1.7 billion people make up 30 per cent of the world's population.

The modern Commonwealth helps to advance democracy, human rights and sustainable economic and social development within its member countries and beyond.

What is the United Nations?

Nearly every nation in the world belongs to the United Nations. Its membership totals 192 countries. When states join, they agree to accept the UN charter. The aims of the charter are:

- to maintain international peace and security
- to develop friendly relations among nations
- to cooperate in solving international problems and in promoting respect for human rights
- to be a centre for harmonizing the actions of nations.

How does the UN work?

Since 2004, the UN mission in Haiti has been working to:

- create a stable and secure environment
- support the development of the political system
- promote human rights.

After the earthquake in 2010, the UN's World Food Programme said that it was collecting enough ready-to-eat meals to feed two million people for the next month.

Pedestrians walk past a ruined building in Port-au-Prince, Haiti

Think about

Why do you think the UN is needed?

The UN tries to ensure that human rights are protected by peacekeeping and helping when disasters occur. Think of a recent example of both these activities.

In the exam

1 Explain why countries want to join the EU.   *2 marks*

2 Which one of the following countries is a member of the Commonwealth?

  A Greenland

  B Spain

  C Australia

  D Japan   *1 mark*

3 Give two different kinds of work carried out by the UN.   *2 marks*

Don't forget!

The European Parliament is not the main decision-making body of the EU. The Council of Ministers makes the decisions.

Raising your grade

'The UN sets the standard for human rights and humanitarian support but governments can ignore it so it is of little use.'

Do you agree with this view?

Give reasons for your opinion, showing you have considered another point of view. You should support your argument with examples wherever possible.

- Does the United Nations Declaration on Human Rights work?
- What happens when countries ignore it?
- What is the UN's role in disaster relief?
- If the UN did not exist, how would human rights be monitored?

On one hand

- The UN Declaration on Human Rights sets the standards.
- Most countries abide by it.
- The UN organizes peacekeeping missions when countries fight each other – or within countries.
- It coordinates disaster relief. It would be difficult for other organizations to do this.

On the other hand

- Many countries ignore the UNDHR.
- The UN does not pass laws so it has no power.
- There are other organizations like the EU and the Commonwealth that could take the role of the UN.

This A-grade student shows a very good understanding of aspects of the course that apply to this question and uses current examples well to build an argument.

Most countries in the world have signed up to the United Nation's mission and the Declaration on Human Rights. It therefore sets the standard for the world. Most countries abide by it and some build it into their own laws. The EU has put together its own version, which is based on the UNDHR and the UK has used this to create its own Human Rights Act.

> This is a very good example of how knowledge and understanding can be used to support an argument.

Its humanitarian work is very important. Soldiers from member countries are called on to help keep the peace. It would be difficult for individual countries to do this on their own. The UN has to make decisions about whether it should try to help when countries fight each other. It does this through the Security Council and countries must vote on each situation.

> Again, the student uses knowledge to justify the point of view.

It is an important coordinator of disaster relief. In Haiti, some of its staff were killed in the earthquake but it quickly got sorted out and became the main organization running disaster relief.

> Current examples are very helpful when it comes to demonstrating that knowledge can be applied.

We need an organization that brings countries together to sort out problems and offer support. It is not an easy thing to do and the UN is not perfect but it would be difficult to think of another way of doing it.

> This sums up the argument well because it demonstrates that the UN is not perfect but there are few alternatives.

On the other hand ...

> Having set a very good case, the student now needs to put the other side of the argument. 'On the other hand' tells the examiner that it is coming next.

3.5 Challenges facing the global community

You will revise

- **The effects of inequality** • **Achieving sustainability**
- **The use of the world's resources** • **Disagreement and conflict** •

Know the facts

In the exam you will be asked questions to test your knowledge of the key facts, so it is really important to learn them. Write a sentence for each of the key facts to show you understand what they mean. You will need to use an example in each sentence, so if you can't think of one – go and look it up!

LEDC

a less economically developed country

MEDC

a more economically developed country

boycott

to refuse to use or have anything to do with something

Fair Trade

a way of buying and selling products that aims to pay the producer a fair price

free trade

trade between countries that is not restricted by things like high taxes on imports

globalization

the increasing interdependence of the world

fossil fuel

a naturally occurring fuel, such as coal or natural gas

global warming

the rise in the average surface temperature of the Earth

Think about

How and why does life in Niger differ from life in the UK?

Can the world be fairer?

	Niger	UK
How much the economy is worth per citizen	$244	$36 509
How fast the economy grew	−0.5%	2.5%
Doctors per 100,000 people	2	230
How long people live	54.5 years	79 years
Number of children dying before the age of five for every 1,000 people	256	7
Internet users per 1,000 people	2	473
Adults who can read	28.7%	100%
Children enrolled in secondary school	8%	99%
International aid	Receives aid	Gives aid
Free education, healthcare and state pensions	No	Yes

Human Development Report 2007/8

The impact of globalization

Why do multinational companies make their products in LEDCs?

Modern technology, combined with improved communication and transportation, has made it easier to trade around the world. Our nations are interdependent. It is not really the countries themselves that trade, but the businesses and consumers within those countries. The importance of trade is likely to increase with advances in technology. Already the internet allows us to buy from anywhere in the world.

There are many people involved in globalization – consumers, employers, large companies and nations. Some businesses have a bad reputation for the way they treat people who are working for them in LEDCs. For example, one UK high street fashion store has 5,000 home workers across the world. They try to monitor conditions but it is very difficult.

Fair Trade or free trade

Would you buy something that you knew had been made in a factory in a country where the people are exploited? Explain why.

Fair Trade is an internationally recognized approach to trading which aims to ensure that producers in poor countries get a fair deal. A fair deal includes a fair price for goods and services, decent working conditions, and a commitment from buyers so that there is reasonable security for the producers.

Achieving sustainability

What are the effects of global warming? How are world organizations trying to overcome the problems? Think of some current examples.

Burning fossil fuels leads to the production of greenhouse gas and is thought to cause global warming. There is pressure for us all to reduce the amount of fossil fuels we use. The Kyoto Protocol is an agreement between many countries to cut their output. The UK has a target of a 60 per cent reduction by 2050. The EU is aiming at 20 per cent by 2020.

Conflict and protest

Civil wars occur when there is conflict within a country. In the late twentieth century, when Yugoslavia fell apart, civil war set in. It was only resolved when the country was broken up and the different groups formed their own nations. There are still problems, for example in Bosnia, where Christians and Muslims live near each other but live very separate lives.

Think about

What sort of problems might lead to civil war? Think of examples of countries where people are at war now.

Mostar Bridge was rebuilt after the civil war but the people on either side lead separate lives.

In the exam

1 What is global warming? *1 mark*

2 What is free trade?

   A A system of trading in which producers always receive a fair share of the value of the final product.

   B A method of trading that is not affected by subsidies on exports and taxes on imports.

   C A system of support given to poor countries by rich countries.

   D A system of trade in which countries exchange goods without paying for them. *1 mark*

3 Why is it cheaper to make consumer goods in China or India than in the European Union? *2 marks*

Don't forget!

Sustainability is often used to refer to the environment – as it does here. Don't forget that it can have a much bigger meaning when referring to communities.

Exam tip

If you do not agree completely with either side of the argument, explain clearly what you think but make sure you come to a clear conclusion.

Raising your grade

'We should try to stop the spread of globalization.'

Do you agree with this view?

Give reasons for your opinion, showing you have considered another point of view. You should support your argument with examples wherever possible.

- How has technology affected globalization?
- What are the advantages and disadvantages of globalization?
- How can pressure groups influence globalization?
- Can governments and international organizations have any effect on globalization?

On one hand

- Globalization is happening because countries are interdependent.
- People in the UK benefit from globalization.
- People in LEDCs can benefit if businesses are responsible.
- Pressure groups involved in Fair Trade help.
- Governments can set standards for production in their countries.

On the other hand

- Globalization can damage local culture.
- Businesses are not always responsible.
- Pressure groups only play a small part.
- If governments make laws to protect employees, businesses can move to other countries.

This answer shows how an A-grade student takes a point of view – but explains that it is not so straightforward and needs some rules to make it work.

I don't think we should try to stop globalization but we need rules to make sure that people are not damaged by it. In the UK, we benefit from trading with other countries. We can have all sorts of food that we cannot grow here. We get things that are made more cheaply in other countries. We do need to make sure that the people in LEDCs are properly protected. There have been many cases where people have been exploited and children have worked long hours for low pay in bad conditions. Most large companies now have codes of conduct that the businesses in LEDCs that supply them are meant to keep, but it can be difficult to monitor them.

Pressure groups can help but they do not protect everyone. Fair Trade works for some suppliers but lots work for companies that do not do Fair Trade products.

It is difficult for international organizations like the UN to deal with the problems that might arise because we do not have international laws. More and more countries are passing laws to protect employees but they fear that businesses will move to countries where there are no laws. Some countries have laws but they are not enforced.

There are people who believe that we should try to stop globalization because ...

The student shows where they stand immediately. This helps the examiner to follow the argument.

This offers good support for the point of view.

Mentioning codes of conduct shows that the student understands how the system works.

This shows that the student understands that Fair Trade isn't the solution to all trading problems.

Using knowledge of current events helps to reinforce the argument.

3.6 The UN, the EU and human rights

You will revise

• **How international justice takes place** •

Know the facts

In the exam you will be asked questions to test your knowledge of the key facts, so it is really important to learn them. Write a sentence for each of the key facts to show you understand what they mean. You will need to use an example in each sentence, so if you can't think of one – go and look it up!

Geneva Convention

an internationally accepted set of rules on the treatment of people in war

International Criminal Court

the Court that deals with the most serious crimes against humanity and with war crimes

European Court of Human Rights

this court was set up to enforce the European Convention on Human Rights

genocide

mass murder of a racial, national or religious group

Think about

Why do you think an International Court of Justice is necessary? The USA, China, Russia and India have not signed up. Why do you think this might be?

What is the International Criminal Court?

The International Criminal Court is the world's first permanent court responsible for prosecuting some of the most serious crimes, such as genocide, crimes against humanity, and war crimes. The aim, in setting up the court, was to create a fair system of justice at the international level that operates according to the rule of law, not according to the whims of politicians, the wealthy, or others who wield power. The Geneva Convention sets out the rules for how people should be treated in war.

Thousands of civilians have fled their burning homes in the Congo while militia groups fight for control.

What are the rules?

Why do you think the EU needs to set down these rights? What effect should it have on the laws in member states?

The European Convention on Human Rights
Right to life
Freedom from torture
Freedom from slavery
Liberty and security
Right to a fair trial
Right to privacy
Freedom of conscience and religion
Freedom of expression
Freedom of assembly
Right to marriage
Freedom from discrimination
Right to redress if rights are infringed

What does the European Court of Human Rights do?

The Court was set up to enforce the European Convention on Human Rights, which had been drawn up by the Council of Europe. The Court can award damages but does not have the power to award other punishments. Ultimately, a country could be expelled from the Council if it did not accept the rulings.

Which court?

The international courts shown below serve different areas and different issues.

Court	Who runs it?	What does it do?
International Criminal Court	Set up by UN but completely independent	Deals with the most serious crimes against humanity
International Court of Justice	UN	Deals with disputes between UN member countries
European Court of Human Rights	Council of Europe	Deals with human rights issues in the 47 member countries of the Council of Europe
European Court of Justice	European Union	Deals with disputes over EU laws

In the exam

1 Name two issues that are dealt with by the International
   Criminal Court.   *2 marks*

2 What is the final sanction of the European Court of
   Human Rights?   *1 mark*

Think about

Think of some examples of cases that have been tried in the European Court of Human Rights.

Give an example of a case in each of these courts.

Exam tip

The question clearly states that you need to put a point of view. If a question is tough, it is easy to waffle about the bits you know. Make sure that you come to a conclusion and put another point of view quite clearly.

Raising your grade

'War crimes should be dealt with in the country where they took place.'

Do you agree with this view?

Give reasons for your opinion, showing you have considered another point of view. You should support your argument with examples wherever possible.

* What are war crimes?
* Will a government, in a country where there have been war crimes, be able to try the guilty?
* Should other nations be able to interfere in the legal affairs of a country?
* Why might an international court be necessary?

On one hand

* War crimes can happen in civil wars.
* War crimes can happen in wars between countries.
* In either case it would be difficult to challenge people who are thought to have committed war crimes.
* In order to overcome bias an international court would be necessary.

On the other hand

* Countries should be independent.
* The USA, Russia, China and India have not signed up because they think the Court might be biased.

War crimes break the United Nations Declaration on Human Rights and the Geneva Convention, which sets the conditions for the treatment of people in war. They include crimes such as genocide and enlisting child soldiers to fight.

It is very difficult for a country to put people on trial for war crimes when one country has been fighting another – or when there has been a civil war. In this situation people are looking for peace and it causes problems in the country. It is also very difficult to get a fair trial when the winning side tries people from the losing side. This means that human rights are being ignored. Sometimes both sides have committed war crimes but only the winning side will have the chance to try the opposition.

Some people think that a country ought to be able to make decisions for itself without interference from others. The USA, China, Russia and India have refused to sign up to the International Criminal Court because they think the judges might be biased. 130 countries have signed up so far – but that leaves a lot that haven't.

As yet, there have been no completed trials in the Court so it is hard to decide how well it is going to work.

I think that ...

> This first paragraph uses the bullet points to help give a clear start to the answer.

> The student is building a picture of the issues related to war crimes trials and human rights.

> The idea of bias is important in Citizenship and very relevant to this question.

> The fact that the student knows that there are no completed trials shows an awareness of events that are current.

> While the student has shown some interesting points, they have not really made a clear statement of a point of view. This needs to come next.

Option A

Environmental change and sustainable development

What's it all about?

This Option gives you the opportunity to explore a range of issues relating to the environment and sustainability. You will need to think about what is happening at the moment. What is going on in the world? Your revision should include making sure that you have good examples and that you are able to look at things from a variety of perspectives. Don't forget all you learnt in Unit 1. The new ideas here build on all you learnt at that stage of the course. Check back on all those facts!

Community
- How can communities take action?
- How can organizations and governments protect people's rights?

Individual
- How can individuals make a difference?
- How can individuals protect people's rights?

National
- What impact does the media have on national policies?
- What is the significance of identities and diversity?

Social
- How do individual and community values affect the issue?

Whose perspectives?

Political
- How do local, national and global green policies affect issues?
- What impact do democracy and justice have in different countries?

Global
- How are LEDCs and MEDCs affected?
- Trade or aid?
- How do different kinds of rights and responsibilities affect individuals and communities?
- What challenges face the global community? Conflict? Inequality? Sustainability?

Ethical
- What is fair and what is unfair?
- How can rights compete and conflict?
- How can hard decisions be made?

What are the issues?

What does ethical mean?

Different people use different words to define 'ethical', but the general view is that it relates to a set of values including compassion, fairness, honesty, respect and responsibility. Working out how to make ethical decisions will help you to decide on your own actions as well as thinking about those of others.

Making ethical decisions

This list of questions will help you to decide.

- Which action results in the most good and least harm?
- Which action respects the rights of everyone involved?
- Which action treats people fairly?
- Which action contributes most to the quality of life of the people affected?

These questions work for all decisions where your actions, or public actions, will affect other people.

A mum and her son choose clothes.

Is everyone's decision the same?

We all have a different set of value judgements, so even when we use the same list of ethical questions, we might come up with different answers.

People have different approaches to quality of life. For example, for some people, living without a car would make life impossible because of a lack of public transport in their area. Others would value eating organic food because they think it makes them healthier – while others can only afford the cheapest food if they are to feed their family. It can be easier for some people to worry about their carbon footprint.

You will revise: **Global warming: the perspectives**

What are the issues?

Is global warming really happening?

Most scientists accept that global warming is caused by the amount of carbon dioxide we pump into the atmosphere. Others don't. They think it is just part of the natural cycle that the Earth has gone through in the past.

What causes global warming?

The scientists who believe in the connection with our activities think global warming is happening because of:

- increasing amounts of greenhouse gases in the atmosphere
- global changes to land surface, such as deforestation
- increasing concentrations of aerosol gases in the atmosphere.

The scientists who believe that the cause is less clear argue that changes in the sun have a greater effect than human activity. They say that the climate has changed over millions of years and we are just in another cycle. In the distant past, there have been ice ages and tropical forests in the UK.

What do people think?

Forty-five per cent of people think global warming is less important than race and immigration, the NHS and crime in terms of national concerns. Locally, they are more concerned about traffic, litter, graffiti, noise and dogs fouling the pavement.

Fifty-one per cent thought it would have little or no effect.

Ninety per cent thought it would have a significant impact on future generations.

Thirty-seven per cent admitted they were doing nothing about climate change.

Seventy per cent thought that the Government should take the lead in combating climate change. It should pass laws to change people's behaviour.

Source: Adapted from Ipsos Mori

Think about

Do you accept global warming is happening? If not, why not? If so, why?

How do you contribute to global warming?

Why do you think people contradict themselves in their views on global warming? Should they take more responsibility?

Don't forget!

Whatever you think about global warming, it is sensible to try to leave the planet as we found it.

What are the issues?

Think about

Should we expect people in India to cut emissions as much as MEDCs?

What are you doing at the moment to reduce your carbon footprint? What more could you do?

What examples of community action do you know about? What sort of help would make it easier for such groups?

What can individuals do?

We can all work to reduce our carbon footprint. First of all, we need to know what it is. The average household in the UK produces 13,999 kg of carbon every year. The average Indian household produces only 1,300 kg. To meet the government targets for 2050, we would need to reduce each household footprint to 5,200 kg. There are many footprint calculators on the web, so check up on yours.

How can you reduce your footprint?

- Ride a bike, or walk.
- Don't buy over-packaged goods.
- Avoid buying plastic – it's hard to recycle.
- Buy environmentally friendly products.
- Recycle all you can.
- Don't buy aerosols.
- Switch off lights.
- Turn the heating down.
- Give old clothes to charity shops.
- Use recycled paper.

Is it better to work together?

There are many environmental projects that involve the community. They might be in a school, the local community or set up by special interest groups, such as looking after ponds or riverbanks.

It takes a bit more effort to be environmentally responsible. When working with others, it is often more fun and people spur each other on to reach targets and achieve the objectives.

The government has set up a system of Community Champions to support local environmental initiatives.

You will revise: *Global warming – not in my backyard?*

What are the issues?

I don't want it here

Many of us claim to care about the environment – unless looking after the environment affects us directly. When it does, we cry 'Not in my back yard!' Wind turbines, tidal barriers and other ways of using less fossil fuel all cause protest from people living nearby.

Are there trade-offs?

Energy-saving light bulbs cost more than traditional ones but they have two benefits. First, they use less electricity and therefore save fossil fuels. Second, they save us money in the long run. There is, therefore, a trade-off when people buy these light bulbs.

Houses can be insulated and therefore lose less heat. The government will give grants to help people install insulation in lofts. This will help the country meet its targets.

How are decisions made?

Local councils and central government have to make decisions about environmental projects like wind farms. They are often faced by vocal protest from 'NIMBYs' and have to work out the best decision for all.

Decisions about the environment often need an ethical framework to help a conclusion to be reached. Have a look at page 74 where you will find the questions that will help you to decide.

Think about

Think of an example of 'NIMBY' activity that you could use in the exam.

Why do you think people protest?

Has your household carried out any energy saving measures that cost money at the beginning but save energy and money in the long run?

Look back to the ethical questions and work out whether an environmental project you know about should go ahead.

Don't forget!

NIMBY means 'Not in my backyard'.

Option A revision questions Part 1

1 Name two values that might be involved in making an ethical decision.

2 marks

2 A carbon footprint is:

1 mark

  A the amount of carbon produced by a car

  B the amount of gas produced in processing carbon dioxide.

  C the sum of all the carbon produced by an individual, organization or country

  D the total sum of methane produced from landfill sites.

3 An opinion is different from a fact because:

1 mark

  A there is always evidence to support an opinion

  B facts are about a wide range of things but opinions are only about politics and religion

  C everyone always agrees with an opinion

  D an opinion is a point of view on an issue.

4 Explain what is meant by NIMBY and give an example.

2 marks

5

View 1:

Most scientists believe that climate change is caused by the increasing amount of carbon dioxide that people pump into the atmosphere. Temperatures have risen as our output of CO_2 has risen.

View 2:

Temperatures haven't been rising for the last ten years but we haven't stopped pumping CO_2 into the atmosphere – so are we really causing global warming? England has been both tropical and covered in ice in the past.

  i Explain briefly what is meant by global warming.

2 marks

  ii There are different views on global warming, although the majority of scientists believe it is happening. Explain why we should look after the environment, even if we are uncertain about global warming.

2 marks

Raising your grade

'People should never protest against decisions to help the environment.'

Do you agree with this view?

Give reasons for your opinion, showing you have considered another point of view. You should support your argument with examples wherever possible.

- Do people have the right to protest?
- Why do people protest?
- Do we need to look after the environment?
- Are public decisions always right?

Exam tip

Make sure that you use your Citizenship knowledge in your writing. It shows the examiner that you are supporting your point of view.

On one hand
- It is important that people have the right to protest in the UK.
- Decision makers need to hear both sides of the argument.
- You need to protect special places.
- You need to protest to protect your own property.

On the other hand
- The environment must be looked after for the future – sustainability.
- NIMBYs just worry about themselves.
- Decisions must be made democratically, not just by those with the loudest voice.

These two points of view are quite extreme so the student needs to work out how to show a sensible point of view that takes ideas from both sides of the argument. This example shows how to use your Citizenship knowledge to build an argument.

The student shows an understanding of the law relating to protest.	In the UK we have the right to protest about things we are concerned about. Protesting does not mean that decisions will be changed. It means putting a point of view. When people care about something, they have the right to tell people their point of view. The people who are making the decision should listen to all points of view and weigh them up and come to a conclusion. As they will have been elected, the decision will be made democratically. If one group is more powerful than the others, and has more money to spend, it can be difficult to get a balance.
This shows an understanding of how public decisions are made in the UK.	
The use of sustainability here helps to build the argument.	Decisions about the environment are difficult because the country must become sustainable but people do not want their lives to change. A wind farm on your doorstep might be noisy and spoil the view, so your house might fall in value. They are concerned for themselves rather than for the community as a whole – but they should still have the right to protest. There have to be some trade-offs if we are going to achieve sustainability.
Trade-offs are important and relate to the ethical perspective. We need to ask: which solution gives the most benefit and the least harm?	I do not agree with the statement, because I believe that people should have the right to protest. However, it is important that decision makers listen to all points of view when they make their decision.

What are the issues?

Think about

Why do you think the emissions trading scheme encourages countries to stay within their limits?

What are the targets?

The EU aims to cut greenhouse gas emissions by 20 per cent by 2020 and increase the use of renewable energy to 20 per cent of the total. It will be done by:

- producing renewable energy
- capturing and storing carbon dioxide
- reducing CO_2 from cars
- revising the European emissions trading scheme – in which countries are set limits but can buy and sell their allowance if they need more or haven't used it all.

Enforcing the rules

Persuasion

Why do you think the rates differ so much? What could be done to persuade people to do more?

Recycling rates have risen steadily but there is still a long way to go. Local and central government tries to persuade us to do better – but it's not easy. Recycling rates vary considerably round the country.

Percentage of household waste sent for recycling
Canterbury City 47.39
Northamptonshire County 46.04
London Borough of Richmond upon Thames 41.73
Ipswich Borough 41.14
Durham County 29.10
Stoke-on-Trent City 26.84
London Borough of Tower Hamlets 19.33

Source: DEFRA

Taxation

People are more easily encouraged to look after the environment if they have to pay for damaging it. For example, people who drive cars that produce high levels of CO_2 pay higher road tax. There are taxes on the amount of waste businesses send to landfill sites.

Taxation can be controversial. Some people claim that it is just a method used by the government to raise more revenue. If all countries do not have the same rules, taxation makes some countries less competitive.

Does everyone agree?

Don't forget!

Targets are easy to set but hard for everyone to reach because we live under different circumstances.

Why is it important for businesses to be able to compete internationally?

The emissions targets are not popular with everyone. The USA, for example, has not signed up to the Kyoto protocol. Reducing the output of gas can be expensive for businesses and therefore makes products more expensive. If countries don't all follow the same rules, this can make it harder to sell the products of countries that obey the rules.

You will revise: Sustainability – local or national?

What are the issues?

Achieving national targets

The UK plans to reduce carbon dioxide emissions by at least 60 per cent by 2050 and at least 26 per cent by 2020, based on levels in 1990. The target will be reviewed to decide whether it should be even stronger.

Emission reductions purchased overseas may be counted towards the UK's targets. This ensures emission reductions can be achieved in the most cost effective way.

Local rules

Businesses in the UK are given a limit to the amount of pollution they can produce. They will have to buy permits to cover each tonne of CO_2 they emit above the cap. They can buy permits from other businesses whose emissions are below their cap. Permits cost about £10 per tonne.

Local authorities are responsible for issuing permits for businesses to pollute. The permit contains ways in which the business must aim to reduce pollution.

Local sustainability

Local Agenda 21 is a 'world-wide action plan' that was agreed to by the United Nations at the Earth Summit in Rio de Janeiro in 1992. It aimed to encourage local authorities to look after their environments. They were asked to create development plans for their communities. These have developed into Sustainable Community Strategies. A sustainable community is likely to:

- be safe and inclusive
- be well planned, built and run
- offer equality and opportunity for all.

It is therefore sustainable in a number of ways – not just environmentally. If a community is to be sustainable, people need jobs and opportunities too. Sustainable communities are all different as communities are all different and one size can't fit all.

Think about

What sort of changes will need to take place if the UK is to meet its targets?

Why will businesses want to avoid buying permits?

What sort of activities might communities get involved in if they are to be sustainable?

Sustainable communities

places where social, economic and environmental activities form a community where people thrive both at home and at work

Don't forget!

Sustainability refers to more than the environment. It includes other things, like helping people into employment and making the community safe.

Local people work to improve their environment.

What are the issues?

The LEDCs argument

The industrialized world developed when no one worried about the environment. The smogs in the UK were infamous – just as they are in Beijing today.

Reducing pollution increases a business's cost of production so the end product will be more expensive and therefore less will be sold. Many LEDCs argue that they should not have to conform to the same rules until their industry is more advanced.

Air polution over Beijing.

What are the trade-offs?

We buy lots of cheap products from LEDCs. They are cheap because:

- people work for lower pay than in MEDCs.
- there are fewer environmental regulations, which makes production cheaper.

We like buying cheap products – but should we think again? If we don't buy them, we might reduce job opportunities for people who may be desperate for work. Clearly, it is not a simple question.

Is there a solution?

It has proved very difficult to find a solution. The 2009 environment summit in Copenhagen failed to reach any real conclusions because LEDCs and MEDCs had different agendas.

One suggestion to solve the problem is to set limited targets for some industries rather then fining countries. In countries where democracy is strong enough, the population may bring pressure on the government to reduce pollution.

You will revise: *Trade or aid?*

What are the issues?

Why do countries grow when they trade?

When one country sells goods to another it makes the country doing the selling richer. People have been employed and paid to make the things that are sold, so they have more to spend so the economy grows. When a country grows there is more money to spend on things like:

- education
- healthcare
- communications.

These all help people to be more productive, so the economy can continue to grow.

Can aid help?

Aid is often needed when there are disasters – when people need food and a roof over their heads. However, aid can also help a country to grow. Governments in MEDCs offer continuing development aid to poor countries. The pie chart shows how UK aid is spent. Unfortunately, some aid never reaches the people it is aimed at because of corruption.

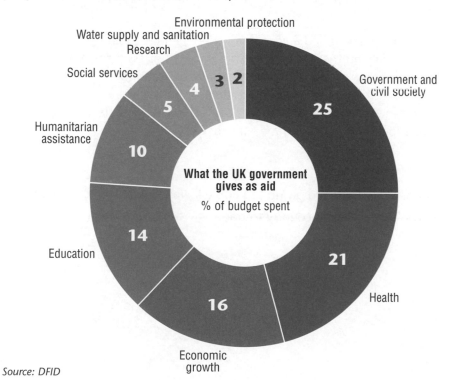

Source: DFID

Do we need both?

Trade will help countries to grow and therefore lift people out of poverty. Aid can help to develop the skills and competitiveness that people need to work and make the products – or provide services – that people in other countries want. Trade and aid can help to ensure that development is sustainable because businesses grow on the basis of having markets to sell their products.

Think about

How do you think education, healthcare and communications help a country to develop?

How can the different ways the UK spends its aid money help LEDCs to develop?

aid

help given by one country to another

Don't forget!

Aid can mean either humanitarian aid – for emergencies – or aid to help the country develop.

Why do countries need both trade and aid?

Option A revision questions Part 2

1 The Kyoto Protocol is:

    A an international agreement about trade

    B an international agreement about the environment

    C an agreement signed by all countries

    D an agreement set up by the European Union.   *1 mark*

2 Which statement best describes a sustainable community?

    A A community that looks after the environment.

    B A community that encourages everyone to join an environmental project.

    C A community in which people thrive at home and at work.

3 Give one advantage of each of the following ways of encouraging people to recycle:

    i persuasion

    ii taxation.   *2 marks*

4 Give two reasons why LEDCs do not want to sign up to environmental targets.   *2 marks*

5

> Trade Aid is a charity based in the UK. It aims to help people in Tanzania.
>
> 'Trade Aid offers training and advice to a variety of local business men and women. Enabling them to develop their own business plans, keep their own profit and loss accounts, and manage their money effectively. Trade Aid also provides inspiration for new ventures and trade opportunities and is able to use its contacts in Dar es Salaam and beyond to expand trade beyond the Mtwara District.'

Source: www.tradeaiduk.org

    i What sort of aid is Trade Aid giving to people in Tanzania?   *1 mark*

    ii Explain how aid can help a country to trade.   *2 marks*

Raising your grade

'Aid is just a waste of money. We need to support trade instead.'

Do you agree with this view?

Give reasons for your opinion, showing you have considered another point of view. You should support your argument with examples wherever possible.

- Are there different kinds of aid?
- What are the objectives of aid?
- Why is aid sometimes wasted?
- What is the relationship between trade and aid?

Exam tip

Sometimes it works well if you put the other point of view first before giving a good, clear explanation of your own. Once you have shown the two points of view, you have at least half marks.

On one hand

- Aid is needed to help in disasters.
- Aid can help a country develop by improving education and health.
- As a country develops it can trade more.
- More trade means more growth and more trade.

On the other hand

- Aid is wasted in corrupt countries.
- Even emergency aid can be misused.
- It would be better to use the money in the UK so we can buy more.

The student sets out another point of view first and then goes on to put her own perspective. It works well in this case and the examiner is very clear about the two points of view.

A good link to other aspects of the course, which shows the student can make such connections.

The awareness that there are problems with aid show that the student understands both sides of the argument.

The student builds on this as the basis for putting her own point of view.

This shows a good understanding of the use of development aid. The following paragraph explains the process well.

A simple and effective conclusion.

The media often tells about how aid is wasted. Even when there are disasters, the headlines often focus on the problems of getting the aid used properly rather than the work that is actually being done. There are cases round the world where aid does not reach the people it is aimed at because there is corruption. It ends up in the hands of people who are already rich. This is clearly not right but when aid helps, it can really make a difference at the local level – and also help the country as a whole.

When aid is aimed at achieving sustainability, it can really make a difference. Providing fishermen with canoes so they can travel further to catch fish is one example of helping communities. Education is often very important because it helps people to get better jobs. This helps a whole country because people with a good education can help businesses to be more competitive in the world. As a result, they will have more things to sell to other countries ...

In the end, countries often need aid to help them to develop trade.

Changing communities: social and cultural identities

What's it all about?

This Option gives you the opportunity to explore a range of issues relating to communities and our identities. You will need to think about what is happening at the moment. What is going on in the world? Your revision should include making sure that you have good examples and that you are able to look at things from a variety of perspectives. Don't forget all you learnt in Unit 1. The new ideas here build on all you learnt at that stage of the course. Check back on all those facts!

Community
- What unifies and divides communities?
- Why are communities complex and changing?
- What encourages community cohesion and brings about change in communities?

Individual
- How can individuals and groups establish identities and deal with diversity?
- What are the different perceptions of being a citizen in the UK?
- What images does the media offer?

National
- What is the effect of national migration policies?
- What is the impact of the media?
- Is the media accurate?
- What connections exist between diverse national, regional, ethnic and religious cultures, groups and communities in the UK?
- How have rights and freedoms been achieved in the UK?

Social
- Why are community cohesion and tolerance important?
- Should there be a balance between rights and responsibilities?

Whose perspectives?

Ethical
- Why is respect important?
- Is it right to limit people's freedom?

Global
- Why do people migrate?
- What are the effects of diversity?
- How are groups in the UK, the rest of Europe and the wider world connected?
- What is the UK's role in the world (with Europe, the EU, the Commonwealth and the UN)?
- What challenges face the global community (including international disagreements and conflict, and debates about inequalities, sustainability and use of the world's resources)?

Political
- What policies and actions address inequalities?
- In a range of contexts, from local to global, what political, legal and human rights and freedoms are there?
- How is information (including that from the media and from pressure and interest groups) used in public debate and policy formation?
- What is the impact of democracy and justice in the UK and other countries?

You will revise: *Making ethical decisions*

What are the issues?

What does ethical mean?

Different people use different words to define 'ethical', but the general view is that it relates to a set of values including compassion, fairness, honesty, respect and responsibility. Working out how to make ethical decisions will help you to decide on your own actions as well as thinking about those of others.

Making ethical decisions

There is a group of questions that will help you to decide.

- Which action results in the most good and least harm?
- Which action respects the rights of everyone involved?
- Which action treats people fairly?
- Which action contributes most to the quality of life of the people affected?

These questions work for all decisions where your action, or public actions, will affect other people.

Are asylum seekers treated fairly?

Is everyone's decision the same?

We all have a different set of value judgements, so even when we use the same list of ethical questions, we might come up with different answers.

People have different views on changes in their communities. They may have lived there for many years and be afraid of change. Others might enjoy the different cultural experiences that immigrants might bring. Some may fear that immigrants will take their jobs. It is important for people to have sound information before they decide on their point of view on an issue about the community.

> **Think about**
>
> Think about a current ethical issue. Work out what you would do and why you would make your decision.

> Choose a current issue that involves a decision about the community. Use the questions to work out what you think you should do.

> **ethical**
>
> relating to a set of values including compassion, fairness, honesty, respect and responsibility

> Think about an issue in your community. Work out why people have different points of view.

What are the issues?

Think about

Why do you think asylum seekers are treated differently from economic migrants?

economic migrant

someone who leaves his or her country to seek a more prosperous way of life

Think about the pros and cons of remittances.

Why do you think the asylum rules have been toughened up?

Asylum seeker or economic migrant?

Refugees have fled from their home country because of war or persecution. They will have applied for asylum but have not yet been given permission to stay. To qualify for asylum in the UK, people must prove they have been persecuted because of their race, religion, nationality, membership of a social group or political opinion, as laid out in the UN Convention on Refugees.

Economic migrants are people who leave their country of origin in order to improve their quality of life. Some pretend to be asylum seekers in order to be able to stay in their chosen country. Others are legal migrants because they come from an EU country

What's the benefit?

Remittances are amounts of money sent home by people from other countries who are working in the UK. Money sent home from MEDCs is the second-largest financial inflow to developing countries. It is greater than international aid. It is estimated to be more than £2 billion. The main recipients are India, Pakistan, the Caribbean (particularly Jamaica), China, Bangladesh, Nigeria and Ghana.

Remittances can make up as much as half of their annual income. The money is spent on basic needs such as clothing, education, food, and health. They are therefore helping achieve the Millennium Development Goals of reducing poverty and expanding access to health and education.

Why do people choose the UK?

The UK has a reputation as a safe and democratic country. Many people in the UK speak English, which is still one of the more widely spoken languages. The Netherlands and France offer better healthcare and benefits but many people still seem to want to come to Britain.

Asylum rules in the UK have become increasingly tough, and the number of applicants has fallen to a quarter of what it was in 2002.

The state of the economy plays an important part. If there are plenty of jobs and wages are high, people want to come here. If unemployment rises, they go home or decide not to come in the first place.

In the exam

Option B revision questions Part 1

1 Name two values that might be involved in making an ethical decision.   *2 marks*

2 Which of the following best describes an asylum seeker?   *1 mark*

    A A person who leaves their country for economic reasons.

    B A person who is looking for a different lifestyle.

    C A person who wants a better education in another country.

    D A person who is fleeing persecution.

3 An opinion is different from a fact because: *1 mark*

    A There is always evidence to support an opinion.

    B Facts are about a wide range of things but opinions are only about politics and religion.

    C Everyone always agrees with an opinion.

    D An opinion is a point of view on an issue.

4 Give two reasons why migrants want to come the UK.   *2 marks*

5

> Unmanned planes are to be used over the English Channel to detect immigrants crossing from France. They are equipped with high-powered cameras and sensors. The Kent police said it would greatly extend the government's surveillance capacity and 'revolutionize policing.'

    i What is an immigrant?   *1 mark*

    ii Give two reasons why immigrants can benefit a country.   *2 marks*

    iii Give two reasons why people might fear the arrival of immigrants.   *2 marks*

Raising your grade

'We should accept anyone who says they will be persecuted if they go home.'

Do you agree with this view?

Give reasons for your opinion, showing you have considered another point of view. You should support your argument with examples wherever possible.

- Should refugees be allowed to stay in the UK?
- Are all asylum seekers genuine?
- Is UK law too harsh?
- What criteria should we use to decide?

On one hand

- We should not send people back to their own country if they will be persecuted.
- We should therefore accept anyone who comes from a country which persecutes people.
- We should check people from other countries because we can't take all the economic migrants too.
- We should use the ethical questions to work it out.

On the other hand

- The UK is already full, so it is difficult to take more people in.
- There are other countries that can take asylum seekers.
- Some people who claim to be asylum seekers are really economic migrants.

This is a sensitive question that can benefit from the use of the ethical questions.

> The student opens by making their point of view very clear. The examiner will now be looking for the other point of view.

I believe that we should accept asylum seekers if they come from a country which persecutes people and they have reasonable evidence that they would be harmed if they returned. There are four questions that helped me decide this.

> The student has used the ethical questions. They have worked through them to develop the argument.

1 Which action results in the most good and least harm?
2 Which action respects the rights of everyone involved?
3 Which action treats people fairly?
4 Which action contributes most to the quality of life of the people affected?

After working through these questions, it does not seem right to send people home if they can show they would be harmed if they returned.

> Here comes the other point of view. The student clearly doesn't agree with it.

Many people think that we are already overcrowded and should not accept anyone else who arrives but this does not seem fair. How would they feel if they were refugees? There are other European countries where they could go.

> Here we have some knowledge to support the argument.

France and the Netherlands do offer better benefits than the UK but people want to come here because they speak the language. If we let them stay, they are more likely to end up working so it would not be too expensive.

> This development shows that the student understands how the situation might develop.

They should be encouraged to improve their English so they do not stay on benefits ...

You will revise: *Is the UK a multicultural society?*

What are the issues?

How different, how similar?

The religious mix in the UK (%)	1996	2006
Christian	52.8	47.5
Non-Christian		
Islam/Muslim	1.8	3.3
Hindu	0.6	1.4
Jewish	0.3	0.5
Sikh	0.2	0.2
Buddhist	0.5	0.2
Other non-Christian	0.4	0.4
No religion	42.6	45.9
Refusal/not answered/didn't know	0.8	0.6

Source: ONS

Think about

Look again at page 10, where you will find a table showing the UK's ethnic mix. How multicultural is the UK?

Living apart – together

There are two definitions of multicultural:

- relating to, consisting of, or participating in the cultures of different countries, ethnic groups, or religions

- supporting integration: advocating or encouraging the integration of people of different countries, ethnic groups, and religions into all areas of society.

The first one suggests that people of different ethnicity and cultures live in the same country. The second one suggests that they integrate.

Are we living in the same country, but not really as one community?

Is multicultural best?

> 'We expect those who come to Britain to play by the rules and to do their best to share in the responsibilities of living together as well as enjoying the rights – for example by learning English so that they can participate fully in the workplace and in the life of the community. And if people want the rules to be different they campaign to change them by the democratic means we have available.'
>
> *Trevor Phillips, Equality and Human Rights Commission*

Trevor Phillips wants us to integrate – rather than living in separate communities. What do you think are the benefits of doing this?

Don't forget!

Multicultural has two meanings: it is often used to describe an integrated community as well as one that is ethnically mixed.

Think about an issue in your community. Work out why people have different points of view.

What are the issues?

What does the law say?

Equal Pay Act	1970
Sex Discrimination Act	1975
Race Relations Act	1976
Disability Discrimination Act	1995
The Employment Equality (Sexual Orientation) Regulations	2003
Employment Equality (Religion or Belief) Regulations	2003
Employment Equality (Age) Regulations	2006

Still in court?

Discrimination at work

A prison officer from Wolverhampton who claimed she was victimized by a male colleague for being attractive has won her claim for unfair dismissal.

Amit Kajla, 22, also won claims for age and sex discrimination against Her Majesty's Prison Service.

During her time at the jail, Ms Kajla claimed she suffered harassment and discrimination from a male prison officer because she was a young and attractive female, working in a mainly male environment.

How does the UK compare?

Men in the UK earn 21 per cent more than women – when looking at gross hourly pay.

The EU average pay gap between the sexes stands at 17.4 per cent. The biggest gap is more than 30 per cent in Estonia, and the smallest – just 4.4 per cent – is in Italy. The EU Commission says it is high time EU governments lived up to the EU's 50-year-old founding principle of 'equal pay for equal work'.

You will revise:
Why do people react differently to immigration?

What are the issues?

How do people react?

Morrissey said …

'Also, with the issue of immigration, it's very difficult because, although I don't have anything against people from other countries, the higher the influx into England the more the British identity disappears so the price is enormous. If you travel to Germany, it's still absolutely Germany. If you travel to Sweden, it still has a Swedish identity. But travel to England and you have no idea where you are. It matters because the British identity is very attractive. I grew up into it, and I find it quaint and very amusing. But England is a memory now. Other countries have held on to their basic identity, yet it seems to me that England was thrown away.'

Fear of change

People are often afraid of change because they fear it will alter their lifestyle. UK culture has been changing for hundreds of years as we have had continuous flows of people from other countries. For example, many big cities have an

area known as Chinatown where many of us go to enjoy a different culture. This is the gate into Liverpool's Chinatown.

Fear of unemployment

Business in the Community says:

The employment of migrant and overseas workers has become an increasing trend. It is widely recognized that valuing diversity helps all organizations to meet their full business and social potential. It is also important that racism is eliminated in the workplace. Failure to tackle this real issue will create unhappy and unproductive working environments, which can only have a negative impact on our economy.

Source: Business in the Community

Think about

Do you think what Morrissey said is true? Give some examples from another point of view.

Think of some examples of how we have built the culture of immigrants into British culture.

Why do you think people fear migrant workers?

What sort of jobs do they often do?

How can migrant workers help the UK economy?

You will revise:
Can problems of community cohesion be resolved?

What are the issues?

Think about

How do you think community cohesion helps people to live together?

How does your school achieve each of these factors? How could it work in the community?

community cohesion

the glue that holds communities together

Don't forget!

Political parties tell us that our society has problems. Keep an eye on policies that are introduced to help people build cohesive communities.

How does the Inspiring Communities Programme help community cohesion? What else might help? Use the ethical questions on page 87 to guide you.

What is community cohesion?

Community cohesion is the togetherness and bonding shown by members of a community. This can be described as the 'glue' that holds a community together. It might include features such as a sense of common belonging or cultural similarity.

What makes communities work?

What makes communities work

Lifestyle
People need education, jobs, a reasonable income, healthcare and decent housing if they are to feel secure in their community.

Social order
If the community is peaceful and secure, people are more likely to respect each other. Lack of social order can lead to suspicion and lack of respect.

Social networks
These connect people and organizations, and help people support each other by offering information, trust and friendship.

Equality
This means that people in the community have equal access to jobs, healthcare and education, for example, which affect people's life chances.

Sense of belonging
It comes from shared experiences, values and identities.

Can we achieve cohesion?

The Inspiring Communities programme aims to support communities to raise the aspirations and educational attainment of young people.

Initially based in 15 neighbourhoods, it will fund and support neighbourhood partnerships to deliver a programme of activities working with young people, their parents and communities, to create new opportunities, broaden horizons and build up the self-confidence of local people. Partnerships responsible for work locally will have at their core schools, councils, third sector organizations, parents and young people. Local businesses and relevant service providers are also encouraged to become involved in the Inspiring Communities initiative.

Source: Communities and local government

In the exam

Option B revision questions Part 2

1 Newspaper reports on immigration are often biased. This means that they:

    A clearly report two or more points of view

    B lean heavily towards a particular viewpoint

    C use complicated language

    D use out-of-date evidence.   *1 mark*

2 Give two features of a cohesive community.   *2 marks*

3 Name two laws that are designed to protect people.   *2 marks*

4 Where we live can greatly affect our opportunities in life. For those living in areas of need, quality of life can be severely limited by what has been called 'postcode poverty'. Government policy aims to improve the quality of life for those living in the most disadvantaged areas by tackling:

    • poor job prospects

    • high crime levels

    • educational under-achievement

    • poor health

    • problems with housing and the local environment.

    i   What is meant by 'postcode poverty'?   *1 mark*

    ii Give two ways in which poor health affects people's opportunities in life.   *2 marks*

    iii Explain two ways in which a community can become more cohesive.   *4 marks*

Exam tip

Remember to provide plenty of evidence for your points of view. The mark scheme asks for this, so you will get higher marks if you do.

'**Integration means that people lose their identity.**'

Do you agree with this view?

Give reasons for your opinion, showing you have considered another point of view. You should support your argument with examples wherever possible.

- Does integration help people to play a role in their society?
- How does integration help a society to be more cohesive?
- Will people forget their own culture if they integrate?
- Is a multicultural society always integrated?

On one hand

- The UK is multicultural but people still live in separate communities.
- They may not be integrated into the community.
- They keep their language and culture.
- They support each other.

On the other hand

- People can integrate and keep their own culture.
- If they integrate, they are more likely to get a good job because they will have learnt English.
- Many young people have achieved this.
- Some older immigrants have also managed both.

Students in different situations might take a different approach to this question. This student takes a balanced view, with plenty of supporting evidence, but comes down clearly on one side.

The student gives supporting reasons for a point of view.

This gives another motivation for the first point of view.

'However' flags to the examiner that another point of view is coming.

Here is supporting evidence of the other point of view.

The conclusion is short but sums up the student's point of view clearly.

People who come to live in the UK often want to maintain their original culture. They may return to their birth country to visit relatives and they still want to fit in there. They need to remember their first language, and their religious and cultural traditions. They want their children to understand all these things, too. Also, people from the same ethnic groups often look after each other. They may fear that if they try to integrate they will lose out on this kind of support.

However, there are examples of communities that have integrated but kept their own identity and culture. The Jewish community has been very successful in doing this – it has integrated fully into education, employment and culture of several countries including the UK, but still practises its own religion and cultural activities. Young people are often very good at integrating, although their families may feel that they have given up aspects of their original culture. They may want to come back to their original culture later...

I feel that it is better to integrate because you can have the best of both worlds. You can make the most of UK society while maintaining your original culture.

Option C

Influencing and changing decisions in society and government

What's it all about?

This Option gives you the opportunity to explore a range of issues relating to the way in which decisions are made and influenced. You will need to think about what is happening at the moment. What is going on in the world? Your revision should include making sure that you have good examples and that you are able to look at things from a variety of perspectives. Don't forget all you learnt in Unit 1. The new ideas here build on all you learnt at that stage of the course. Check back on all those facts!

Community
- How are decisions different and how are they made in different ways in different communities?
- What impact and consequence do individual and collective actions have on communities, including in the voluntary sector?
- What is the impact of identities and diversities?

Individual
- How can individuals participate in decision-making, either personally or in groups?

National
- What are the national influences on public opinion and national decisions and how are they influenced by the impact and accuracy of the media?
- What development and struggle has there been for different rights and freedoms in the UK (speech, opinion, association and the vote)?
- How does parliamentary democracy operate in the UK?

Whose perspectives?

Social
- Who is responsible for decisions and what redress is there?
- What is the balance between rights and responsibilities?

Political
- Whose opinions matter most?
- Who represents us and who is accountable for decisions?

Global
- How do global events and moral considerations influence decisions and the economy?
- How do other forms of government, both democratic and non-democratic operate beyond the UK?
- What is the impact of democracy and justice in the UK and other countries?

Ethical
- What is fair resource allocation and distribution?
- How are people's contribution to society and government affected?

What are the issues?

Think about

Think about a current ethical issue. Work out what you would do and why you would make your decision.

Choose a current issue that involves a decision on a national or local issue. Use the questions to work out what you think you should do.

ethical

relating to a set of values including compassion, fairness, honesty, respect and responsibility

What does ethical mean?

Different people use different words to define 'ethical', but the general view is that it relates to a set of values including compassion, fairness, honesty, respect and responsibility. Working out how to make ethical decisions will help you to decide on your own actions as well as thinking about those of others.

Making ethical decisions

There is a group of questions that will help you to decide.

- Which action results in the most good and least harm?
- Which action respects the rights of everyone involved?
- Which action treats people fairly?
- Which action contributes most to the quality of life of the people affected?

These questions work for all decisions where your action, or public actions, will affect other people.

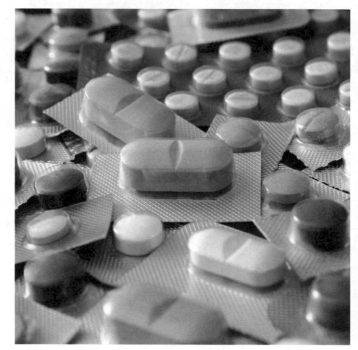

Should all drugs be available through the NHS?

Is everyone's decision the same?

Think of a current issue – such as the use of speed cameras or sentencing for criminals. Why might people have different views about these issues?

We all have a different set of value judgements, so even when we use the same ethical questions, we might come up with different answers.

People have all sorts of views on the decisions that are made about the way we live. These can range from the way the legal system works, to decisions made about the economy. In order to explore these ideas, we need to look at how public opinion is formed and the influence that it can have.

You will revise:
How individuals and groups can influence change

What are the issues?

Ways to bring about change

There are all sorts of ways to bring about change. Here are some of them:

- using individual determination
- being a role model
- persuading our elected representatives
- using the legal system
- breaking the law in order to intimidate people.

Think about

How did change take place in the example below? Think of an example of each of the other ways of changing things.

Judges ruled against freezing assets

A landmark decision by seven Supreme Court justices ruled that ministers acted unlawfully in imposing financial restrictions on individuals without a vote in Parliament. They allowed a challenge by five men, convicted of terrorism, whose assets had been frozen.

Individual or group?

People often join pressure groups if they want to protest about an issue. A pressure group usually has a louder voice and is harder to ignore. A group is therefore more likely to be effective and bring about change.

How are the people in the picture aiming to bring about change? Think about a current example of people campaigning for change.

Is change for the better?

It all depends on your perspective. Whether it's a question of a new supermarket in town, the building of a bypass or joining the Euro, people will never all agree. In the end the decision-makers must weigh up the alternatives and work out a solution that will be best for most people and hurt the least.

Work out the perspectives relating to the decision to increase security at airports.

What are the issues?

Think about

Think of some examples of decisions made at each level of government.

Local, national or international

- Local government makes decisions that affect the local area. In London, the boroughs all have their own councils. In other big cities, there is one council that represents the city as a whole. Other parts of the country have county councils or district councils.

- The government in Westminster makes national decisions.

- International decisions are made by the Council of Ministers of the European Union. These decisions affect all the member countries and national governments have to comply.

How does political change happen?

Why do people decide to vote a different party into power at a general election?

Once in power, a government can make decisions about all aspects of running the country but ministers must always remember that they are accountable to the electorate who can decide whether to re-elect them at the end of the term of office. This period can be no more than five years.

The government can be taken to task because they haven't kept all their promises. This may affect how people decide to vote at the next election. Sometimes circumstances change, so it would be unreasonable to expect the government to keep all the promises it makes. The recession, which resulted from the banking crisis, meant that the government had to spend more than it planned. This meant that there was less to spend on other things. In circumstances like these it may be impossible to do everything that was promised.

What about a referendum?

Think of the advantages and disadvantages of making decisions through referenda.

We very rarely hold referenda in the UK. The last one was over joining the EU in 1975. Other countries use them more frequently. Switzerland often consults its population in this way. Recently they voted to ban the building of minarets on mosques.

You will revise: **How changing the electoral system would lead to change in how we are governed**

What are the issues?

Decisions: local or national?

There is much debate about how local government should be and it will always be hard to satisfy everyone. Here are some of the arguments.

On one hand:

- Having many layers of government is expensive.
- Some decisions have to be made nationally.

On the other:

- Better decisions can be made about a local area – at a local level.
- People feel more in touch with local government.

Should we have proportional representation?

The London Assembly.

In the UK, nearly all elections are 'first past the post'. This gives an advantage to large parties and makes it hard for small ones to get representation.

The Liberal Democrats would like to see the introduction of proportional representation as this gives more seats to smaller parties. The London Assembly elections use a method of proportional representation.

The outcomes give a fairer share of seats to all parties but can make it hard to govern because there is less likely to be one dominant party in power.

What about EU decisions?

Countries can choose the electoral method they want to use in EU elections, so there is a great mix. In the UK we use proportional representation in these elections. The turnout in the EU elections in the UK is very low.

> **Think about**
>
> What sort of decisions do you think should be made locally, nationally and internationally?

> Why do you think it can be hard to govern if there are lots of small parties in parliament?

> **Don't forget!**
>
> There are many kinds of proportional representation. The main ones are single transferable vote, party list and the alternative vote.

> Why do you think the turnout is low for EU elections in the UK? Can you suggest what might be done about it?

Option C revision questions Part 1

1 Name two values that might be involved in making an ethical decision.   2 marks

2 An opinion is different from a fact because: 1 mark

   A there is always evidence to support an opinion

   B facts are about a wide range of things but opinions are only about politics and religion

   C everyone always agrees with an opinion

   D an opinion is a point of view on an issue.

3 A decision to bring a new law into force in the UK is taken by: 1 mark

   A the government

   B the general public

   C government ministers

   D voters.

4 Name two legal ways in which individuals can work to bring about change.   2 marks

5

> 'One of the main arguments advanced in favour of some form of proportional representation is that it will make everyone's vote count in some way, and therefore give more people an incentive to vote.'

   i   Explain briefly what is meant by 'proportional representation'.   2 marks

   ii Name one disadvantage of proportional representation.   1 mark

   iii Name one advantage and one disadvantage of the 'first past the post' system.   2 marks

Raising your grade

'Local decisions should be made locally.'

Do you agree with this view?

Give reasons for your opinion, showing you have considered another point of view. You should support your argument with examples wherever possible.

- What sort of decisions can be made locally?
- What sort of decisions should be made nationally?
- Are there any decisions that can't be made locally?
- How do people feel if decisions are all made centrally?

Exam tip

By setting out the two points of view at the beginning, you show the examiner that you deserve at least half marks straight away.

On one hand

- People are more likely to vote if they can see the effect of their decision.
- People who do not live in the area can't know enough to make decisions about it.
- People should have a say about how taxes are spent in their local area.

On the other hand

- Some decisions about a local area have to be made nationally so things are the same across the country – such as education
- Even when there is a local effect, some decisions must be made nationally – such as military decisions.
- Fewer people vote in local elections than national ones.
- Local taxes may not provide enough money for big initiatives.

The student sets out a point of view and then demonstrates why it doesn't work, so the other point of view is up front.

The student makes clear from the beginning that they understand that there is another point of view.

People are usually more willing to get involved if they can see the effect of their actions. This means that they might vote more often. Unfortunately, this doesn't really seem to work because turnout is lower in local elections than national elections. It could therefore be argued that decisions should all be made nationally because more people have been involved in selecting the government.

Here the student is showing an understanding of democracy and the relationship between the number of voters and decision-making.

Clearly, there are some very local decisions that central government doesn't have time to deal with – so they should be made locally. Planning decisions, for example, should be made locally. A supermarket chain wanted to build a new store near where I live – but it was rejected. The supermarket appealed to central government and was given the go-ahead. I wonder why we bothered to run a big campaign against it when no one listened.

A good practical example. This shows that the student has made the connections between real, local events and Citizenship.

Schools are local but it is important that education is organized centrally so we all get the same standard – so it needs to be planned centrally. Main roads need to be looked after centrally so that the national network works.

This demonstrates the difficulty of separating local and national decisions. The student gives a good reason to support the argument.

I think we need to work out which decisions can be taken locally as some things are standard across the country.

What are the issues?

Fact or fiction

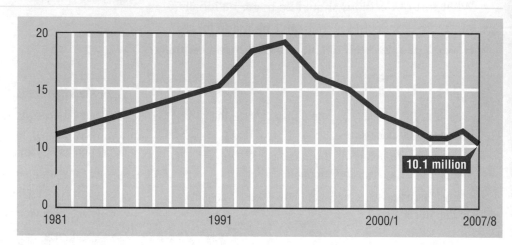

Trends in crime – incidents (millions)
Source: Home Office

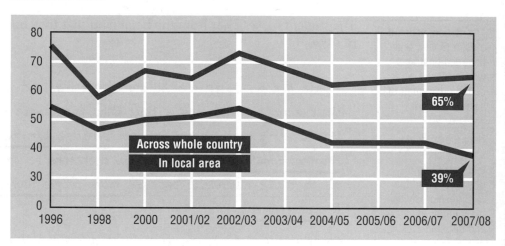

Perception that crime is rising – % perceiving more crime
Source: Home Office

The impact of the media

People make their impressions of the world around them from newspaper headlines and TV news – even if they don't read the paper or listen to the whole programme. They can therefore have a distorted view of the world.

The effect on society

- People can be detained for 28 days without being charged with a crime.
- Laws now restrict our rights to free speech and meeting in non-violent groups.
- People's DNA is being kept on record.
- Our right to protest has been seriously limited. For example, people can no longer protest close to the Houses of Parliament.

Source: Adapted from Liberty

You will revise:
Whether the UK sends too many people to prison

What are the issues?

The role of prison

People have different views about the purpose of prison. It could be for:

- punishment – keeping people locked up?
- prevention – keeping people off the streets?
- rehabilitation – helping people deal with the outside world?
- revenge – enabling victims to get their own back?

What's the effect of prison?

Prison makes it more difficult to function in the outside world because:

- it breaks contacts with families and friends
- a prison record makes it harder to get a job
- education in prison may not be adequate
- people get out of the work habit
- people lose the skills of organizing themselves.

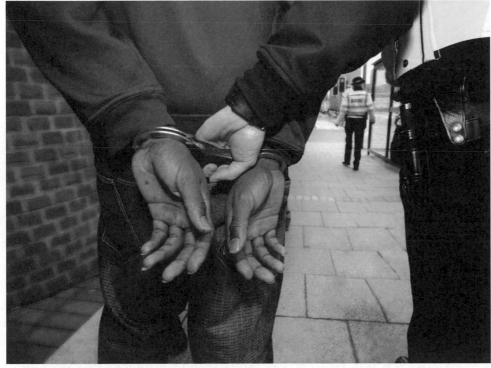

The re-offending rate for young people is over 75 per cent

How does the UK compare?

The UK has more recorded crime per head of its population than any other country in Europe – except Sweden. But it sends nearly twice as many people to prison per head of population than Sweden. You have to be careful with the data though, because different countries record it in different ways.

Think about

What do you think prison should do for people if they are to be able to take part in society when they leave?

Work out how these factors make it difficult for people to function in the outside world.

Don't forget!

The effect of the media is important in all sorts of issues. Many newspapers have strong views on prison and sentencing – and influence people's views.

What alternatives are there to prison?

What are the issues?

Think about

Think of some examples of civil and criminal cases.

What's the difference?

Criminal

- The state prosecutes the defendant
- Defendants have to prove they are not liable
- The burden of proof for criminal offences is that of 'beyond reasonable doubt'
- The penalties for criminal offences are fines and imprisonment, as well as other non-custodial punishments

Civil

- One person can claim redress from another person
- The defendant is innocent until proven guilty
- The burden of proof is 'the balance of probability', which is much lower than for criminal matters
- The penalty is paying damages or being prevented from doing something. You can't be sent to prison

Why use civil law?

Think about

What sort of law is used in each of these cases? What does each type try to achieve?

John Terry applied for an injunction to stop the media reporting his affair with his team-mate's ex-girlfriend.

The treasurer of a youth football club was accused of stealing thousands of pounds from the Oxfordshire club.

What's the cost?

How do you think the cost affects people's decision about whether to go to law?

- If you are the victim of a criminal offence, the state prosecutes and you don't have to pay for the case to take place. If you are the defendant, you will have to pay for your defence – and there is little financial help from the state.

- If you are the victim in a civil case, you have to pay for your defence and there is little help from the state. The defendant also has to pay their way. The person who loses will have to pay all the costs of the case.

Don't forget!

The penalties for the two types of crime are different. You can't be sent to prison by a civil court.

You will revise:
Are privacy and civil liberties in decline?

What are the issues?

How are we protected?

Our privacy and civil liberties are protected by:

The United Nations Declaration on Human Rights …

UNDHR Article 12

No one shall be subjected to arbitrary interference with his privacy, family, home or correspondence, nor to attacks upon his honor and reputation. Everyone has the right to the protection of the law against such interference or attacks.

UNDHR Article 3

Everyone has the right to life, liberty and security of person.

The European Convention on Human Rights …

The right to live, as far as one wishes, protected from publicity.

Are they in decline?

The government says that we need to give up some of our rights if we are going to be safe and has changed the law to protect us from terrorism. Liberty, the human rights pressure group, wants these issues to be looked at very carefully before we decide where to draw the line.

What are the trade-offs?

When new laws are passed, it is important to work out how they might be used in future. For example, if the government can monitor emails, it might want to do so for reasons other than those related to terrorism. It is also important to consider the effect on society in general. For example, sections of the population who feel they are being targeted by such laws may be alienated.

> **Think about**
>
> How do you think these statements contradict today's laws and events?

> Think of examples of laws that have changed to protect us from terrorism.

> Use the ethical questions on page 98 to work out whether the government should be allowed to monitor our emails.

107

What are the issues?

How does each of these groups affect the way we think?

How is public opinion formed?

We are surrounded by information. It comes from

- pressure groups
- the media
- political parties
- government.

Together these all influence what we think. Our friends and family have an effect too.

The ear of government?

What are the dangers when the government is persuaded to take action because it wants to be popular?

Public opinion can be powerful. There are dangers in this, though. The loudest voice isn't always right, so the government has to think carefully before being influenced. There is an argument that says we live in a democracy and elect our government, so it should have a free hand until the next election. However, new situations arise and there are occasions when listening would be useful.

A government can be persuaded because it wants to be popular. The media can drive new legislation. The News of the World campaigned for people to be told whether known paedophiles lived in their area. The government decided to allow people to check up on individuals. It became known as 'Sarah's Law', after a little girl who was abducted and murdered.

Riot police protect the Houses of Parliament from a demonstration

Don't forget!

The government is the party that has won most seats in the election and therefore forms 'the government'. Parliament is made up of all the MPs of all parties.

Who decides?

What factors do you think help the government to decide whether or not to be influenced by public opinion?

The government has the final say. It must weigh up the alternatives because it has a limited amount of money to spend. Public opinion can also call for the law to be changed in ways that would infringe people's human rights – so everything must be considered carefully.

You will revise: **Who controls our economy?**

What are the issues?

The role of government

The government has to make decisions about how it runs the economy. It does this through the budget when it sets tax levels and decides how to spend its money. Interest rates are also used by the Bank of England to influence how we spend money. It does not always have a completely free hand because there are some influences that are hard to control – like the credit crunch of 2009.

The EU

The UK has more control over its economy because we do not use the Euro. In countries that do use the Euro, the interest rates are fixed. We can put them down if we want people and businesses to spend more, and up if we want them to spend less. This happens because higher interest rates make borrowing more expensive.

The impact of multinationals

Very large companies can make decisions that affect the economy. If company tax is increased above other countries, a business might decide to move production to a country where the overhead costs are lower. Equally, they can be attracted by a business-friendly regime. They can also sell products more cheaply than businesses that produce in the UK.

How are countries connected?

Trade connects us to the rest of the world, so changes elsewhere can affect our economy. When people grow anxious about the state of the economy they often reduce their spending – which has a knock-on effect for businesses and other people. Unemployment will then rise and people will have less to spend – so we are in a cycle. These connections are both national and international.

For example, when oil prices rise it makes everything more expensive because transport and production becomes more expensive – and household costs rise.

How do petrol price rises affect the household budget?

Think about

What is happening in the economy at the moment? How does it affect the decisions the government makes?

Who benefits and loses when interest rates change?

How can multinationals affect the UK economy?

How does economic uncertainty affect people and countries?

Don't forget!

Remember that the economy is always changing. It's not just about governments – you affect what is going on by choosing to spend or to save.

In the exam

Option C revision questions Part 2

1 Newspaper reports on crime are often biased. This means that they:

   A clearly report two or more points of view

   B lean heavily towards a particular viewpoint

   C use complicated language

   D use out-of-date evidence.   *1 mark*

2 Give two examples of ways in which crime has led to laws that reduce our freedom.   *2 marks*

3 What are the differences in the costs of a civil and a criminal case?   *4 marks*

4 Give two ways in which the government can control the economy.   *2 marks*

5

> A vicious dog attack in Bradford in 1991 left six-year-old Rukhsana Khan with appalling injuries that shocked the nation and media pressure pushed the government into drawing up the Dangerous Dogs' Act. Fifteen years on, it has become increasingly clear that that hurriedly drafted legislation is deeply flawed. Horrific dog attacks on children as well as adults still regularly happen.

   i What is meant by 'media pressure'?   *1 mark*

   ii Why did the government bring in the new law?   *1 mark*

   iii Explain how the following can influence public opinion:

      a pressure groups

      b political parties.   *4 marks*

Raising your grade

'The government should bring in strict laws to protect us from terrorism.'

Do you agree with this view?

Give reasons for your opinion, showing you have considered another point of view. You should support your argument with examples wherever possible.

- Do we need protecting from terrorism?
- What laws have been passed to protect us?
- How do these laws affect our freedom?
- What does the United Nations say about our human rights?

Exam tip

You need to develop an argument to do well in the long answers, but if you want to get a top grade you must also support it with knowledge and examples.

On one hand

- Terrorism hurts people so we need protection.
- The government must protect us – whatever it takes.
- The government must justify its actions.
- It will know if the public accept the changes when there is an election.

On the other hand

- We will never remove the risk.
- We need protection but we need to balance the impact of laws with our human rights.
- We must be careful with new laws because other governments might use them differently.
- Perhaps the terrorists have won when new laws make our lives more complicated.

This student shows that they have been picking up a lot of current information during the course. This helps to reinforce their argument and points of view.

The opening paragraph shows the student has a good understanding of changes in legislation.

Here the student shows that they have been keeping up with changes that are taking place.

Connections are important in Citizenship and this shows an understanding of the relationship between the UN and EU.

The argument is well supported by an example. This helps the student to move to the next level.

Again, this shows the student is up to date.

The government has brought in many laws and changed the rules on people going through airports to protect us from terrorism. Also, people can be detained for 28 days without being charged with a crime. Laws now restrict our rights to free speech and meeting in non-violent groups. Our right to protest has been seriously limited. People's DNA is being kept on record.

The government has been taken to the European Court of Human Rights because it has changed the law on keeping DNA. Although this was for crime in general, it also supports the government's campaign against terrorism. The Court found that the UK was breaking the European Convention on Human Rights – and it was told to change UK law to meet the requirements.

If our law breaks the EU convention, it also breaks the UN Declaration on Human Rights, but this isn't binding on countries as there is no penalty for breaking it.

We definitely need protecting but I do agree with the statement that we will never stop it. Every time the rules are changed, terrorists just find another way of getting round the rules. Body scanners have been introduced to stop people getting on planes with explosives that don't show up on the normal machines.

Answers to 'In the exam' questions

Unit 1 Citizenship Today

Theme 1
Rights and responsibilities

1.1 Community and identity

1 People coming to live in the UK from other countries.

2 C

3 D

1.2 Human, legal and political rights

1 The right to take part in elections and other democratic activities.

2 An MP sits in the House of Commons. An MEP sits in the European Parliament.

3 Government by the people, either directly or through elected representatives, for example in a general election, local election, European election or bi-election.

1.3 Development and struggle

1 They can take their case to the European Court of Human Rights.

2 The right to vote.

1.4 Rights and responsibilities of consumers, employers and employees

1 Equal opportunity to work.

2 A

3 A type of court dealing only with disagreements over employment laws.

Theme 2
Power, politics and the media

2.1 How the media informs and influences public debate

1 B

2 D

3 Slander is saying something incorrect about a person and libel is putting it in writing.

2.2 How the media informs and influences public opinion

1 Questioning a sample of the population to build a picture of the views of the public on a particular topic.

2 A

3 In order to present the public with good stories about the government in the hope of being re-elected.

2.3 The justice system

1 A group of people who decide if someone is guilty in a court of law.

2 A barrister speaks for a client in court. A solicitor gives advice to a client and may speak in court.

3 B.

2.4 The voice of democracy

1 A pressure group usually deals with a single issue – like the environment or human rights. A political party has policies that deal with everything a government has to tackle – from the economy to transport, education and health.

2 A type of democracy where citizens have the right to choose someone to represent them on a council or in Parliament as an MP.

3 Young people feel that their voice is being heard. They are more likely to vote when they reach 18 because they have been involved at an earlier age.

2.5 The role of democracy

1 The area represented by an MP.

2 An MP is elected to represent an area of the country – a constituency. A Secretary of State is an MP who has been selected to run a government department such as the Treasury, Health or the Environment.

3 A Bill is a proposal for a new law. An Act is a bill that has been passed by Parliament and has become a law.

2.6 Does democracy work?

1 All those who are registered to vote.

2 C

3a A country where the leader makes all the decisions with no reference to the population.

3b One of the two following points:
- People have no say in how the country is run.
- It often means that people's human rights are disregarded.

Theme 3
The global community

3.1 Achieving sustainability

1 There are several reasons, for example we produce too much carbon dioxide and use forms of non-renewable energy.

2 Wind power, tidal power, hydro-electric power.

3 LA 21 is a UN initiative that requires local councils to develop strategies to improve sustainability. This might include encouraging walking buses for school children or helping people to be more energy efficient.

3.2 The economy at work

1 A general rise in prices.

2 If the government spends money in ways the electorate like, they are more likely to vote for the party at the next election.

3 By retraining people, the government helps people to find new jobs, especially if their old jobs are no longer needed.

3.3 People's impact on the community

1 Organizations with a social purpose that do not aim to make a profit.

2 Two from: meeting people, to learn new skills, to help me with my career.

3.4 The UK's role in the world

1 To be able to trade freely with other member states, or to benefit from the grants which the EU gives to help development.

2 C – Australia

3 Peace keeping, disaster relief, protecting human rights.

3.5 Challenges facing the global community

1 The rise in the average surface temperature of the Earth.

2 B

3 Because labour and/or the running costs of a factory are usually lower.

3.6 The UN, the EU and human rights

1 Genocide, crimes against humanity.

2 Being thrown out of the Council for Europe.

Unit 3 Citizenship in Context

Option A
Environmental change and sustainable development

Revision questions Part 1

1 Any two of the following: compassion, fairness, honesty, respect and responsibility.

2 C

3 D

4 It stands for Not In My Backyard. People protest to protect their own interests, for example about wind farms. There are environmental protesters in a variety of places. Choose one you know about.

5 i Global warming is the rise in the average surface temperature of the Earth.

ii We should leave the planet as we found it so as not to disadvantage people in the future.

Revision questions Part 2

1 B

2 C

3 i One of the following: People need encouragement to recycle. They will feel a greater sense of personal responsibility and involvement in their community.

ii If people are taxed, they are more likely to do as required because they will lose money if they don't.

4 Two of the following:

- MEDCs developed before anyone was concerned about the environment so they had an advantage.

- It costs more to produce things when taking account of the environment so it might reduce employment in these countries.

- Because it costs more, other countries might not buy the products – so development would be slowed.

5 i Development aid.

ii • It can educate people so they have the skills to help the country produce more and export more. This helps the country to grow

- It can provide better healthcare – and healthy people contribute more to the economy.

- It can improve communications. Better transport links help trade. Electronic communications would also help development.

Option B
Changing communities: social and cultural identities

Revision questions Part 1

1 Any two of the following: compassion, fairness, honesty, respect and responsibility.

2 D

3 D

4 Two from: safety, jobs, lifestyle, may have the same language.

5 i A person who moves into a country to live there.

ii Skills, work others don't want to do, culture, different food.

iii They fear immigrants might take jobs, or bring in aspects of an unfamiliar culture.

Revision questions Part 2

1 B

2 Two of the following: social order, good social networks, a sense of belonging, equality, a decent lifestyle.

3 Two of the following:
- Equal Pay Act
- Sex Discrimination Act
- Race Relations Act
- Disability Discrimination Act
- The Employment Equality (Sexual Orientation) Regulations
- Employment Equality (Religion or Belief) Regulations
- Employment Equality (Age) Regulations.

4 i Areas where quality of life is poor.

ii Two of the following:
- If people can't attend school they may get a poor education.
- If people can't work they will have to depend on benefits.
- Some people with poor health can't join in all aspects of society, e.g. some may have a limited social life.

iii Two of the following: by improving education, by improving housing, by developing a safe community.

Option C
Influencing and changing decisions in society and government

Revision questions Part 1

1 Any two of the following: compassion, fairness, honesty, respect and responsibility.

2 D

3 A

4 Any two of the following: by using individual determination, by being a role model, by persuading our elected representatives, by using the legal system.

5 i An electoral system in which the number of seats a party wins is roughly proportional to its share of the vote.

ii One of: many small parties in Parliament, weak government, difficult to make policy happen.

iii Advantage: the government usually has the power to put its policies into effect. Disadvantage: the number of seats don't represent the number of votes.

Revision questions Part 2

1 B

2 Any two of the following:
- People can be detained for 28 days without being charged with a crime.
- Laws now restrict our rights to free speech and meeting in non-violent groups.
- People's DNA is being kept on record.
- Our right to protest has been considerably limited.

3 Criminal: the state prosecutes and you don't have to pay for the case to take place. If you are the defendant, you will have to pay for your defence.

Civil: you pay for your defence. The defendant has to pay their cost. The person who loses will have to pay all the costs of the case.

4 Through changes in taxes and government spending. Interest rates are also used – through the Bank of England.

5 i Newspapers and TV campaigning for change.

ii To persuade the public to vote for them at the next election.

iii A Pressure groups campaign through public events, the media and their membership to try to change public opinion.

B Political parties have a manifesto, and use leafleting, party political broadcasts and appearing in the media to try to change public opinion.

GCSE
Citizenship
Edexcel

Exam practice workbook

Jenny Wales

How to use this workbook

How the workbook is organized

This exam practice workbook is designed to help you prepare for the Edexcel GCSE Citizenship exams. It aims to help you develop your exam skills and test how well you are doing with your revision. You can use it to work out what you are good at and where you need to do more revision to improve your grade.

If you are doing the Short course, you need to practise for the Unit 1 exam. If you are doing the Full course, you need to practise for both the Unit 1 and the Unit 3 exams.

There are three options to choose from in the Unit 3 exam. You need to answer questions on only one of these options, so make sure you know which one you are doing.

This workbook links closely to the pattern Units 1 and 3 of Edexcel GCSE Citizenship Studies, as shown in the table below.

Units 2 and 4 are assessed by controlled assessment. This Workbook only covers your practice revision for the two examined units – Units 1 and 3.

Unit 1	Citizenship Today 1 hour	Three themes: • Rights and responsibilities • Power, politics and the media • The global community.	40% of short course 20% of full GCSE
Unit 2	Participating in Society	Controlled assessment	40% of short course 20% of full GCSE
Unit 3	Citizenship in Context	Three options (of which you choose **one**): • Environmental change and sustainable development • Changing communities: social and cultural identities • Influencing and changing decisions in society and government.	40% of short course 20% of full GCSE
Unit 4	The Campaign	Controlled assessment	40% of short course 20% of full GCSE

Skills you will need in the exam

Each exam paper is a mix of the following types of question. This Workbook gives you examples of each kind to try, so that when you come to do the exam you will have had plenty of practice. Nearly all the questions are based on source material – words and images that are provided with the question. You will be asked to read the source material carefully to help you to answer the questions.

Multiple-choice questions

These test your knowledge, to help you make sure you know the facts.

Short-answer questions

These often ask you for definitions or to identify the answer from the given source material. They might also ask you to explain something. If you have worked carefully through the Revision Guide, you should find these very straightforward.

Extended writing

You will be asked to write longer responses to some questions. The marks available for these questions range from 6 to 15. The questions that are worth fewer marks may ask you to explain something in just a bit more detail than a short-answer question. The questions that are worth more marks will expect longer answers – they will ask you to discuss two sides of an argument and come to a conclusion. In the exam, you must make sure you do as these questions ask. If you don't, the examiner can't give you more than half marks for that question.

Checking your progress

As you work through the practice questions, you can check how well you are doing by looking at the 'exam practice' answers that are given at the end of the workbook.

However, please remember that the extended writing questions can be tackled in different ways – there isn't just one 'correct' answer. Compare your answers with the examples given in the answers section to see if you are working along the right lines. Try not to look at the answer to a question before you have completed it.

In the answers section you will also find tables showing the assessment levels that the examiners use when marking the exam papers. You can use the tables to think about how you can achieve the highest level possible when you answer a question.

Your use of English is assessed in the questions that are worth 12 or 15 marks. The levels tables also show how use of English is assessed.

Section A

Some questions must be answered with a cross in a box ☒. If you change your mind about an answer, put a line through the box ☒ and then mark your new answer with a cross.

Make sure that you answer *all* the questions in Section A.

In the exam, you are advised to spend no more than 40 minutes on this section.

Theme 1: Rights and responsibilities

1 Study Source A below.

Source A

Full body scanners introduced at airports

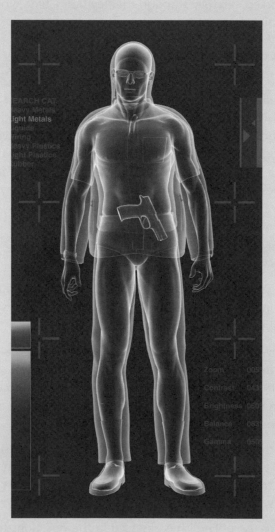

Full body scanners at Heathrow and Manchester airports have caused outrage among civil liberties campaigners. They claim the scanners, which act like a mini radar device 'seeing' beneath ordinary clothing, break the law under the Human Rights Act. Air passengers who refuse to submit to a full body scan at Heathrow and Manchester airports could be barred from taking their flights.

The Equality and Human Rights Commission (EHRC) warned that using personal characteristics could single out Muslims, Asians and black people for scanning at airports. This would break the discrimination laws.

A government spokesperson said 'We must use every piece of technology to prevent terrorists from creating more atrocities.'

Alex Deane, a barrister and director of campaign group Big Brother Watch, said such measures meant 'the terrorists have won'.

a) According to Source A, which human rights are being broken?

    ☒ A Freedom from slavery

    ☒ B Equality before the law

    ☒ C Right to privacy

    ☒ D Freedom of speech   *(1 mark)*

b) Using Source A and your own knowledge, state two reasons why people object to the full body scanners.

1 _____

_____

2 _____

_____ *(2 marks)*

c) Using Source A, name two of the laws that the Equality and Human Rights Commission think could be broken when selecting people to be scanned.

1 _____

_____

2 _____

_____ *(2 marks)*

d) According to Source A, Big Brother Watch is a:

    ☒ A political party

    ☒ B pressure group

    ☒ C charity

    ☒ D business.   *(1 mark)*

e) Explain why Alex Deane said that 'the terrorists have won'?

_____

_____

_____

_____

_____

_____ *(2 marks)*

Now study Source B, below.

Source B

Sacked Honda worker wins case

Nick Bradley had worked at the Honda car plant for eight years until he was dismissed for gross misconduct.

He was a 'checker' on the production line but didn't notice that a robotic arm that applied sealant to car roofs was not working. He failed to check 124 cars – which cost Honda about £35,000 to repair.

Mr Bradley said he had been dismissed unfairly because he had not been trained properly and did not know about all the checks he was expected to carry out.

The employment tribunal agreed with his claim of unfair dismissal.

The amount of compensation that Honda had to award to Mr Bradley must be decided within 28 days.

f) According to Source B, why was Nick Bradley's claim successful?

_____

_____ *(1 mark)*

g) An industrial tribunal:

- ☒ A is organised by groups of employers
- ☒ B is organised by trade unions
- ☒ C deals with disputes between employees and the government
- ☒ D deals with disputes between employers and employees. *(1 mark)*

h) According to Source B, why was Nick Bradley given compensation?

_____

_____ *(1 mark)*

i) Name one course of action a business must carry out before dismissing someone.

_____

_____ *(1 mark)*

j) Give two ways in which a trade union helps employees.

1 _____

_____

2 _____

_____ *(2 marks)*

Theme 2: Power, politics and the media

2 Study Source C below.

> **Source C**
>
> # Gordon's just out to catch the vote of the elderly
>
> Gordon Brown's getting desperate for votes. He's announced that a 'National Care Service' for the elderly will be set up if the Labour Party is returned to power after the election.
>
> The Prime Minister pledged that every pensioner who leaves hospital would be offered help at home for four to six weeks. More than 500,000 elderly patients are re-admitted to hospital each year.
>
> The Conservatives asked how the government would pay for the extra care. The spokesperson said he was amazed that the Labour Party had done nothing like this in all the years they've been in power. They claimed that the pledge was only made to attract older people to vote Labour at the election.

a) i   Using Source C, write out one statement in the first paragraph that is only an opinion.

Opinion

_____

_____ *(1 mark)*

ii   Using Source C, write out one statement in the second paragraph that is only a fact.

Fact

_____

_____ *(1 mark)*

b) Using Source C, give two reasons why the newspaper article is biased against Gordon Brown and the Labour Party.

1 _____

_____

2 _____

_____ *(2 marks)*

c) The prime minister:

☒ A is the leader of the government

☒ B is the leader of the opposition

☒ C decides whether laws should be passed

☒ D decides who should be in Parliament.

d) What is the document that a political party produces before an election to tell people its plans?

(1 mark)

_____

_____ *(1 mark)*

e) Give one way in which the government raises the money to pay for things like care for the elderly.

_____

_____ *(1 mark)*

Now study Source D below.

Source D

Will technology change elections?

Turnout in general elections has fallen to its lowest for 75 years. There have been many suggestions of ways to increase the number. Some people thought that the internet would change representative democracy for ever. Everyone could vote on everything at the touch of a button. This would encourage more people to take an interest in politics. It would also be much cheaper than current elections.

f) Using Source D, give two reasons why some people think that online voting on all issues would be a useful innovation.

1 _____

_____

2 _____

_____ *(2 marks)*

g) What is meant by 'turnout'?

_____

_____ *(1 mark)*

h) 'Everyone could vote on everything at the touch of a button' is a quote from Source D.
What term is used to describe this method of decision making?

_____

_____ *(1 mark)*

i) Give two reasons why it is important for people to vote in elections.

1 _____

_____

2 _____

_____ *(2 marks)*

Theme 3: The global community

3 Study Source E below.

Supporting sustainable development

During the war in Uganda tens of thousands of children were abducted to fight for the Lord's Resistance Army. Other children were born in the refugee camps and have known no life outside them.

The Northern Uganda Youth Development Centre in Gulu is a Commonwealth-supported project dedicated to helping young people readjust after twenty years of civil war in the region. It offers training in a range of subjects, including basic business and life skills. Up to 140 students are currently receiving tuition in subjects such as tailoring and metal work. Many of them walk miles to attend classes.

A teacher guides two students in the tailoring class at the Northern Uganda Youth Development Centre

Youth unemployment and lack of education and skills will affect the future of Northern Uganda. Many students hope to get work and earn enough money to return to school. Education was severely disrupted during the war.

People are now returning to their villages and the camps are closing down. Projects like this are encouraging sustainable development.

Adapted from www.thecommonwealth.org

a) According to Source E, the Northern Uganda Youth Development Centre is a project supported by:

☒ A the Commonwealth

☒ B the United Nations

☒ C the government

☒ D a charity. *(1 mark)*

b) The Commonwealth is:

☒ A a group of countries ruled by Britain

☒ B a voluntary group of countries that trade together

☒ C a voluntary group of independent countries

☒ D a group of countries that have the same laws. *(1 mark)*

c) Which of the following is not an objective of the Commonwealth?

☒ A a source of practical help for sustainable development

☒ B building global agreement

☒ C develop democracy

☒ D peace keeping.   *(1 mark)*

d) Using Source E, give two ways in which the project is supporting sustainable development.

1 _____

_____

2 _____

_____   *(2 marks)*

e) Using Source E, name two ways in which these young people have been deprived of their human rights.

1 _____

_____

2 _____

_____   *(2 marks)*

f) Using Source E and your own knowledge, explain the effect that youth unemployment and lack of education and skills will have on people in Northern Uganda.

_____

_____

_____

_____   *(2 marks)*

g) Source E gives an example of sustainable development. Give two other ways in which countries can achieve sustainable development – apart from those that improve environmental sustainability.

1 _____

_____

2 _____

_____   *(2 marks)*

In the exam you will be required to choose *only one* question to answer from Section B. Of course, for revision purposes, you may want to attempt them all.

In the exam you are advised to spend no more than 20 minutes on Section B, so it is good practice to aim to complete your question within 20 minutes when you are revising.

4 Theme 1: Rights and responsibilities

'In the UK we live together – but separately.'

Do you agree with this view? Give reasons for your opinion, showing you have considered **another point of view**.

To answer the question above, you could consider the following points and other information of your own.

- What is a 'multicultural society'?
- What are the advantages and disadvantages of living in a multicultural society?
- Do different communities really live together?
- Should communities be more integrated?

(12 marks)

OR

5 Theme 2: Power, politics and the media

'You should never break the law.'

Do you agree with this view? Give reasons for your opinion, showing you have considered **another point of view**.

To answer the question above, you could consider the following points and other information of your own.

- Why do we have laws?
- Should we obey them because they are made democratically?
- In what circumstances might people break the law?
- Is it ever right to break the law?

_____

_____

_____

_____

_____

_____

_____

_____

_____

_____

_____

_____

_____

_____

_____

_____

(12 marks)

OR

6 Theme 3: The global community

'The government should take complete responsibility for solving global warming.'

Do you agree with this view? Give reasons for your opinion, showing you have considered **another point of view**.

> To answer the question above, you could consider the following points and other information of your own.
>
> - Why is global warming a problem?
> - What does the government do to deal with global warming?
> - Can governments deal with it alone?
> - What responsibilities do individuals have?

_____

_____

_____

_____

_____

_____

_____

_____

_____

_____

_____

_____

_____

_____

(12 marks)

Based on questions by Edexcel Ltd.

Option A Environmental change and sustainable development

Source A: World-wide Carbon Dioxide Emissions 2006/7

In 2006/7 the list of countries with the highest carbon dioxide emissions differed when the countries were listed by emissions per head of population.

	Total Emissions (%)	Rank Order in World		Rank Order per Head of Population
China	22%	1st	USA	9th
USA	20%	2nd	Canada	10th
Russia	6%	3rd	Russia	33rd
India	5%	4th	Japan	35th
Japan	5%	5th	Germany	36th
Germany	3%	6th	UK	41st
UK	2%	7th	China	91st
Canada	2%	8th	India	130th

Source: adapted from http://en.wikipedia.org

1   Which country listed in Source A is 5th in rank order of total carbon dioxide emissions and 35th when measured by head of population?

☒ A Russia

☒ B Japan

☒ C India

☒ D UK.

(1 mark)

Source B: 10 new nuclear power stations for the UK – but is nuclear the answer?

In 2009 the government announced plans to build ten new nuclear power stations as a substitute for worn-out power stations. However, the UK's Sustainable Development Commission says nuclear power is **not** the whole answer. It says:

- More nuclear power stations will help to stabilise CO_2 emissions.
- They will widen the UK's range of energy sources.
- However, even doubling the UK's nuclear capacity would only cut CO_2 emissions by 8% by 2035.
- Nuclear fuel is limited in supply so strictly it is not sustainable.
- It is expensive, if not impossible, to dispose of nuclear waste safely in the long term.
- If the UK has a new nuclear programme, other countries might want the same. This might lead to accidents, radiation exposure and terrorist attacks.

Source: adapted from http://www.treehugger.com

2   According to Source B, new nuclear power stations are being built because:

   A they are cheaper than other sources of power

  B nuclear fuel is sustainable

  C they are safer than other forms of power

  D they will widen the UK's range of energy sources.   *(1 mark)*

Sailesi Vaheke's beehive could produce up to 50 bottles of honey. Photo credit: Elvis Sukali/Oxfam.

In Malawi, the UK's Department for International Development is helping millions of people to afford essentials like seeds and fertiliser.

- In Thyolo District, ten beehives were provided, along with bee-keeping equipment and training in how to produce honey.

- Each beehive can produce 50 bottles of honey, so the villagers should make over $700 at each harvest.

- 'The money from the sale of the honey will raise the people's living standards as they can purchase fertiliser and boost their other crop harvests next season' says Sailesi Vaheke of the local beekeeping group.

Source: adapted from http://www.dfid.gov.uk/

3   According to Source C, bee-keeping will:

☒ A improve people's diet

☒ B give people an income of $1,200

☒ C help people to buy fertiliser and seeds

☒ D help fertilise the crops.

(1 mark)

Source D: Severn Barrage proposed to make sustainable energy

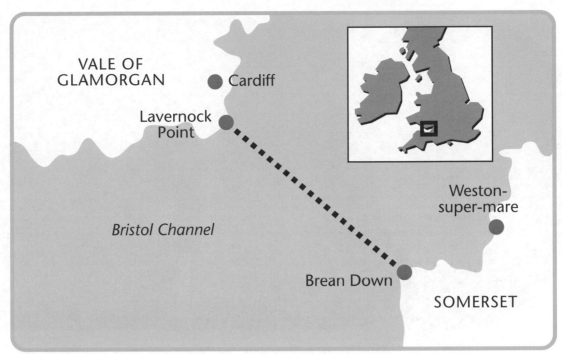

A Severn Barrage using tidal power to make sustainable energy has been proposed. Water would be captured behind a dam in the river estuary. It would flow through the gates as the tide goes out. This would drive turbines that generate electricity.

- The River Severn has a 14 metre difference between water levels at high and low tides. This makes the turbines generate a great deal of electricity.

- The government hopes to harness the power of the Severn to generate electricity.

- Many groups are concerned about the environmental impact of these proposals.

- Bristol-based pressure group *Stop the Barrage Now* say that the barrage could cost over £15 billion.

- They say the barrage would add to local flooding, reduce fish stocks, damage bird life as well as ruining mudflats across an area of more than 77 square miles.

Source: adapted from http://www.climateandfuel.com, http://www.guardian.co.uk, and http://www.carboncommentary.com

4 According to Source D, the pressure group, *Stop the Barrage Now*, does not want the barrage to be built because it will:

   ☒ A damage bird life

   ☒ B generate more electricity

   ☒ C increase fish stocks

   ☒ D solve flood problems. *(1 mark)*

5 Tidal power is renewable because:

   ☒ A it can produce unlimited amounts of electricity every day

   ☒ B it can generate energy without using up any resources

   ☒ C it produces more energy than other forms of power generation

   ☒ D it produces less energy than other forms of power generation. *(1 mark)*

Source E: Who do you support – the Nimby or the Dimby?

Jonathan Dimbleby used to protest against windfarms. He now plans to build a small wind turbine in his meadow in Devon, upsetting his NIMBY neighbours.

- Jonathan's wind turbine will provide his family with all the electricity they need in their home.
- It will stand about 15 metres high, but will be out of earshot and largely hidden from the village by the surrounding trees and hedges.
- His neighbours Bob and Marinella Hollies see things very differently. Bob says they were plagued by noisy neighbours before they moved to their favourite corner of Devon.
- They valued the quietness and the views of rolling countryside.
- Their garden is a haven for wildlife.
- They think Jonathan's turbine will be an eyesore.

Source: adapted from http://www.mailonsunday.co.uk

6   According to Source E, Jonathan Dimbleby's neighbours do not want the wind turbine to be built because:

☒ A it will provide all the power he needs for his home

☒ B they think it is an eyesore

☒ C it is hidden from the village by a hedge

☒ D it will increase the output of sustainable energy.   *(1 mark)*

7   The statement in Source E 'It will stand about 15 metres high' is a fact rather than an opinion because:

☒ A it was reported in a newspaper

☒ B the neighbours think it is 50 ft high

☒ C it cannot be proved to be correct

☒ D it can be proved to be correct.   *(1 mark)*

8 Using Source A, explain briefly why China produces more carbon dioxide than any other country but is only 91st in the list showing rank order per head of population.

_____

_____

_____

_____ *(2 marks)*

9 Source B says that 'More nuclear power stations will help stabilise CO_2 emissions'. Briefly explain what is meant by this statement.

_____

_____

_____

_____ *(2 marks)*

10 Source C says that aid to develop bee-keeping will improve living standards and promote trade. Explain why this is the case.

_____

_____

_____

_____ *(3 marks)*

11 Aid is one way of helping less economically developed countries. Explain how effective aid might be.

_____

_____

_____

_____

_____ *(6 marks)*

12 a) Give two reasons why the UK should be investing in sustainable energy.

1 _____

_____

2 _____

_____ *(2 marks)*

b) Give two reasons why less economically developed countries object to cutting their carbon emissions.

1 _____

_____

2 _____

_____ (2 marks)

13 a) What is global warming?

_____

_____ (1 mark)

b) Give two causes of global warming.

1 _____

_____

2 _____

_____ (2 marks)

14 Do you agree that our emissions of carbon dioxide should be controlled by taxation and laws rather than relying on our sense of responsibility?

Give reasons for your opinion, showing that you have considered **another point of view**.

_____

_____

_____

_____

_____

_____

_____

_____

_____

_____

_____

_____

_____ (8 marks)

15 'Looking after the environment is more important than the rights of individuals.'

Do you agree with this view?

Give reasons for your opinion, showing that you have considered **another point of view**.

> You could consider the following questions and other information of your own in your answer:
>
> - Is it important to look after the environment?
> - What sort of environmentally friendly developments will help the environment?
> - Why do some people object to environmentally friendly developments?
> - How should a decision be made about whether such developments can go ahead?

_____

_____

_____

_____

_____

_____

_____

_____

_____

_____

_____

_____

_____

_____

_____

_____

_____

_____

Continue overleaf

(15 marks)

Option B Changing communities: social and cultural identities

Source A: Funeral cortege and crowd at Wootton Bassett

Every time a fallen serviceman or woman is brought back to the UK, their bodies are taken from nearby RAF Lyneham along the High Street of Wootton Bassett.

- At the beginning, a handful of people stood silently with their heads bowed.
- Now large crowds of locals and relatives gather to show respect.
- Most people now think of Wootton Bassett when they hear about service men and women who have died abroad.

Source: adapted from http://www.mirror.co.uk

1 In Source A, the crowds of people in Wootton Bassett could be described as a community.
Which of the following is the best description of a community?

☒ A A group of people who are tolerant of others.

☒ B A community where people have different interests.

☒ C People who live near each other.

☒ D A group of people who share a common interest.

(1 mark)

Source B: Tony Blair talks about the duty to integrate and share British values

Britain's values are completely different compared with 30 years ago.

- We now have tough laws outlawing discrimination and racism has largely been kicked out of sport.
- Diversity is valued by an increasing number of people.
- A recent MORI opinion poll found that only 25 per cent of Brits say they would prefer to live in an all-white area.

Only 12 per cent of whites would mind if a close relative married a black or Asian person, barely a third of the figure at the end of the last century.

Source: adapted from http://www.number10.gov.uk and http://reportingfrombelgium.files.wordpress.com

2 Using Source B, an opinion poll is:

    ☒ A an annual questioning of people by the government

    ☒ B questioning a sample of the population on a particular topic

    ☒ C using people's opinions to make laws

    ☒ D using people's opinions to select representatives.   *(1 mark)*

3 In Source B, Tony Blair was at the time the Prime Minister of the UK. The Prime Minister is:

    ☒ A the leader of the opposition

    ☒ B the UK's representative in the European Union

    ☒ C the leader of the majority party in the House of Commons

    ☒ D the president of the UK.   *(1 mark)*

Source C: Multicultural Leicester

Highcross shows what a multicultural community there is in Leicester. People with different ethnicities and cultures share their festivals, religions, music and foods.

• They make lifelong friends in the city's schools, colleges and universities and at work.
• People from different backgrounds follow local sports teams and share leisure activities.

In a café in the shopping centre, you can hear different languages being spoken while Lucy swaps places with Anita on their baby-sitting rota so she can play in the netball team. While this is going on, Lucy's dad, who owns the café, plays chess with Anita's brother, Amir. He is a soldier serving with Lucy's husband Gary.

4   Using Source C, the best explanation of a multicultural community is one that is made up of:

 ☒ A different cultural or ethnic groups

 ☒ B British citizens

 ☒ C people who all speak English

 ☒ D people who come from other countries. *(1 mark)*

Source D: Main reasons for international migration in 1997 and 2007

Here are some of the reasons why people migrate to or leave the UK each year.

	1997, UK (thousands)			2007, UK (thousands)		
	Inflow	Outflow	Balance	Inflow	Outflow	Balance
Definite job offer	63	88	-25	172	100	72
Looking for work	41	51	-9	71	73	-2
Accompany/join friends/family	74	62	12	85	43	42
Formal study	87	15	72	149	15	134

Source: adapted from Office for National Statistics (ONS)

5   According to Source D, in 2007 most of the balance of people arriving and leaving the country was highest in the following category:

    ☒ A definite job offer

    ☒ B accompany/join friends/family

    ☒ C formal study

    ☒ D looking for work.   *(1 mark)*

6   The figures in Source D are fact rather than opinion because:

    ☒ A they were printed in a newspaper

    ☒ B they were the result of an opinion poll

    ☒ C they were produced by a political party

    ☒ D they were prepared by an independent body.   *(1 mark)*

Source E: Campaigning to save Toxteth Street

There are plans to replace terraced houses in Toxteth Street (East Manchester) with new energy-efficient, cheap-to-maintain homes that will give the area a 'new start'. These are opposed by the *Save Britain's Heritage* pressure group and local residents, who say that:

- improving the houses would be cheaper than rebuilding
- improving will save millions of tons of carbon dioxide being released into the atmosphere
- the local street pattern gives the community its distinctive character and should be preserved
- the families know each other, feel safe in the area and like the community spirit as everyone looks out for each other.

Source: adapted from http://www.savebritainsheritage.org

7   According to Source E, local residents want to save Toxteth Street because:

☒ A the community has a distinctive character

☒ B there is plenty of work in the area

☒ C the houses are energy efficient

☒ D the houses are cheap to maintain.   *(1 mark)*

8   State two ways in which the people of Wootton Bassett, in Source A, are showing respect for the fallen service men and women who pass through the town.

1 _____

_____

2 _____

_____   *(2 marks)*

9   In Source B, Tony Blair says we have tough laws to combat discrimination and racism. Name three different laws that combat different types of discrimination.

1 _____

_____

2 _____

_____

3 _____

_____ *(3 marks)*

10 In Source B, Tony Blair says that diversity is valued by an increasing number of people. Give two ways in which people might show that they value diversity.

1 _____

_____

2 _____

_____ *(2 marks)*

11 Source C shows how a town can make the most of its multicultural community. Using Source C and your own knowledge, what would be the most effective ways a town could help to create a successful multicultural community?

_____

_____

_____

_____

_____

_____

_____

_____

_____

_____

_____

_____

_____ *(6 marks)*

12 a)   What is the difference between an asylum seeker and an economic migrant?

1 _____

_____

2 _____

_____ *(2 marks)*

b)   The rules for migrants coming into the UK have become tougher in recent years. Give two ways in which the rules have changed.

1 _____

_____

2 _____

_____ *(2 marks)*

13 a)   In source E, 'Save Britain's Heritage' is referred to as a pressure group. What is a pressure group?

_____

_____ *(1 mark)*

b)   Explain the difference between a pressure group and a political party.

_____

_____

_____

_____ *(2 marks)*

14   Using Source E and your own knowledge, do you agree that Toxteth Street should be pulled down?

Give reasons for your opinion, showing that you have considered **another point of view**.

_____

_____

_____

_____

_____

_____

_____

Continue overleaf

_____

_____

_____

_____

_____

_____

_____

_____

_____

_____ _(8 marks)_

15 'If everyone in the country is integrated, we will all lose our cultures.'

Do you agree with this view?

Give reasons for your opinion, showing that you have considered **another point of view**.

You could consider the following points and other information of your own in your answer:

* To what extent do you think the UK could be said to be 'integrated'?

* How does a mix of cultures affect the UK?

* If everyone learns English, will people lose their original culture?

* What effect does a mix of cultures have on British culture?

_____

_____

_____

_____

_____

_____

_____

_____

_____

(15 marks)

Source A: Historic day as Youth Parliament takes over House of Commons Chamber

In October 2009, over 300 elected Members of the Youth Parliament (MYPs) aged 11–18 from all parts of the UK took over the House of Commons chamber for their annual meeting.

- It was the first time anyone other than MPs had debated in the Commons and sat on the green benches.
- 109 MYPs spoke on issues of concern to young people.
- Members included 50 per cent female, 22 per cent from ethnic minorities and 3 per cent were young people with disabilities.
- After debating five issues the MYPs voted to decide their campaigning priority for 2009/10.
- The votes for each issue were:
  - University education being free: 56
  - Youth crime and how to tackle it: 34
  - Free transport for young people: 54
  - Job opportunities for young people: 62
  - Lowering the voting age to 16: 107.

Source: adapted from http://www.climateandfuel.com, http://www.guardian.co.uk, and http://www.carboncommentary.com

1 Source A refers to MPs. An MP is a person elected to:

   ☒ A the local council

   ☒ B the House of Commons

   ☒ C the European Parliament

   ☒ D the Welsh Assembly.

(1 mark)

Source B: Birmingham project uses TV Secret Millionaire cash to fund move

A Birmingham project has celebrated a £20,000 donation from Kavita Oberoi, one of Channel 4's 'Secret Millionaires'.

- Kavita spent 10 days undercover with three community groups, only revealing her true identity at the end of the show.

- She then donated a total of £45,000 to two struggling groups that serve local people – including £20,000 to the Karis Neighbourhood Scheme.

- Ten months later, she returned to see the new premises that her money had provided.

- Karis's Manager Linden Sanders said that when Kavita gave us the cheque she said she wanted us to move to a bigger location so we could help more people.

Source: adapted from http://www.birminghammail.net

2   Source B refers to the Karis Neighbourhood Scheme. This is:

☒ A a voluntary organisation

☒ B a trade union

☒ C a pressure group

☒ D a political party.   *(1 mark)*

Source C: Families which do not get enough help from the government

To mark the launching of the new Family Commission in 2009 by national charity 4Children, a *YouGov* opinion poll asked over 2,000 adults which types of family, in their opinion, do not get enough help from the Government:

- 25% said families with children
- 61% said families with elderly relatives
- 35% said families in crisis
- 49% said families with disabled members.

Source: adapted from www.thefamilycommission.org.uk

3 Source C refers to an opinion poll. An opinion poll:

    ☒ A always gives an accurate view of public opinion

    ☒ B tells the government which laws to pass

    ☒ C tests the opinion of a sample of the public

    ☒ D tests the opinion of everyone in the country.   *(1 mark)*

4 Using Source C, the majority of people who responded to the opinion poll wanted the government to help:

    ☒ A familes with disabled members

    ☒ B families with children

    ☒ C families in crisis

    ☒ D families with elderly relatives.   *(1 mark)*

Source D: Protesters save seven post offices from axe

Seven London post offices have been spared the axe following angry protests against their closure.

- One branch was kept open after local campaigners pointed out that it served a block of 50 flats for the visually impaired.

- Local MP Greg Hands, who had met Post Office bosses said: 'I am delighted the Post Office has seen sense and local people have had their say'.

- He added: 'The government shouldn't have been pushing through this closure programme in the first place'.

Source: adapted from www.thisislondon.co.uk

Counter measure: local residents protest against the closure of Alexandra Park Road post office, one of 155 due to be shut across London.

5 Source D refers to campaigners. They would have set up a:

☒ A political party

☒ B community group

☒ C pressure group

☒ D business. *(1 mark)*

6 Which of the following statements from Source D is opinion?

☒ A Seven London Post Offices have been spared the axe.

☒ B It served a block of 50 flats for visually impaired people.

☒ C Greg Hands met the Post Office bosses.

☒ D The government shouldn't have been pushing through this closure programme. *(1 mark)*

Source E: Changing prisoners for the better

Grendon is no ordinary prison. New inmates are surprised to be called by their first names and not to have to wear prison uniforms. About 70 per cent of them sign up for a tough programme of therapy and rehab. They say:

- 'I want to understand why I'm violent, why I'm angry, why I'm on drugs.'
- 'You have to be honest with yourself if you want to change.'
- 'Coming here makes you face your actions.'

Grendon has very low rates of:

- assaults
- drug use
- self harm
- re-offending.

Kvetch, *by Michael Lester, HM Prison Grendon, Ariane Bankes Outstanding Award.*
Image courtsy of Koestler Arts Trust.

Despite its success, Grendon is not an expensive prison to run. It may well be better value for money than most mainstream jails – partly because fewer prisoners re-offend.

Source: adapted from www.communitycare.co.uk

7   According to Source E, Grendon has low rates of reoffending because:

☒ A it is expensive to run

☒ B prisoners have to wear uniform

☒ C prisoners do not have therapy

☒ D it helps people face their actions. *(1 mark)*

8   Using Source B and your own knowledge, give two reasons why people do voluntary work.

1 _____

_____

2 _____

_____ *(2 marks)*

9 Source C gives four ways in which the government helps families. Name two ways in which the government raises money to support families.

1 _____

_____

2 _____

_____ *(2 marks)*

10 In Source D, people protested to keep their Post Office open. Name two other methods they might have used and explain why they might be effective.

Method 1 _____

_____

_____

Method 2 _____

_____

_____ *(4 marks)*

11 Using Source E and your own knowledge, explain why people who go to prison are more likely to re-offend than those who receive community sentences.

_____

_____

_____

_____

_____

_____

_____

_____

_____

_____

_____

_____ *(6 marks)*

12 a) Give two ways in which opinion polls can influence decision making.

1 _____

_____

2 _____

_____ *(2 marks)*

b) Explain why opinion polls are not always accurate.

_____

_____

_____

_____ *(2 marks)*

13 a) The opinion poll in Source C suggests how the government should spend its money.
Name one factor that influences the government's decision.

_____

_____ *(1 mark)*

b) The government is accountable to the electorate. Explain what is meant by accountable.

_____

_____

_____

_____ *(2 marks)*

14 Using Source A and your own knowledge, do you agree that people should be able to vote at 16?

Give reasons for your opinion, showing that you have considered **another point of view**.

_____

_____

_____

_____

_____

_____

_____

_____

_____

_____

_____

_____

_____

_____

_____

_____

_____ *(8 marks)*

15 'The government must stop reducing our privacy and compromising our human rights.'

Do you agree with this view?

Give reasons for your opinion, showing that you have considered **another point of view**.

You could consider the following points and other information of your own in your answer:

- What are our human rights?
- How important are our human rights?
- We must be protected from terrorism, so does that mean human rights take second place?
- Does the government need to know what people are doing, in order to keep us safe?

_____

_____

_____

_____

_____

_____

_____

_____

_____

(15 marks)

Glossary

Accountable: if you are accountable for something, you are responsible for it and have to explain your actions.

Act: a law passed by Parliament.

Advocacy: arguing on behalf of a particular issue.

Aid: help given by one country to another.

Assembly: a body of people elected to decide on some areas of spending in a region.

Asylum seeker: someone who has applied for protection as a refugee and has not yet been told whether they will be accepted.

Barrister: a lawyer who represents and speaks for their clients in court.

Bias: to favour one thing over another unfairly.

Bill: proposal to change something into law.

Boycott: to refuse to use or have anything to do with something.

British nationals: citizens of the United Kingdom.

The Budget: the processes each year when the Chancellor of the Exchequer explains how the government will raise and spend its money.

Business rates: a form of tax paid by all the businesses in an area. The amount a business pays depends on the rent that could be charged for their premises.

Cabinet: a group of MPs who head major government departments. Meets weekly to make decisions about how government policy will be carried out.

Canvassing: when people try to persuade others to vote for their party in an election.

Carbon footprint: Our individual carbon footprint is the sum of all the emissions of carbon dioxide caused by our activities in a given period.

Censorship: limiting the information given to the general public.

Chancellor of the Exchequer: the member of the government who is responsible for the country's finances.

Citizens Advice Bureau (CAB): an organization that offers free advice on consumer and other legal matters.

Civil law: this covers disputes between individuals or groups. Civil law cases are often about rights.

Commonwealth of Nations: a voluntary group of independent countries.

Community: A group of people who are in close contact and who share common interests and values.

Community cohesion: the glue that holds communities together.

Compensation: making amends, something given to make good a loss.

Constituency: the area represented by an MP.

Consumer: a person who buys goods or services for their own use.

Contract of employment: a document that details an employee's and employer's responsibilities for a job.

Convention: an agreement, often between governments.

Council: a group of people who are elected to look after the affairs of a town, district or county.

Council tax: a tax paid by everyone who lives in an area. It is based on the value of their house.

Councillor: a member of a local council, elected by people in the area.

County court: a local court that has limited powers in civil cases.

Criminal law: this deals with offences such as murder and drug dealing. Cases are between the Crown Prosecution Service (acting for all citizens) and the offender.

Crown Court: courts held in towns in England and Wales where judges hear cases.

Cultural diversity: The range of different groups that make up a wider population.

Customs Duty: taxes on products bought from other countries.

Data Protection Act (DPA): a UK law designed to protect personal information that is stored on computers or in an organized paper filing system.

Declaration: a document setting down aims and intentions.

Deflation: the general fall in prices.

Democracy: government by the people either directly or through elected representatives.

Devolution: the transfer of power from central to regional government.

Dictatorship: a country's leader makes all the decisions with no reference to the population.

Discrimination: treating someone less favourably because of their colour, ethnic origins, gender or disability.

Dismissal: when an employer ends an employee's contract of employment ('sacking').

Division of labour: where employees concentrate on a particular task or job at which they are expert.

Dual heritage: if you have parents or recent ancestors of different origins.

Economic growth: when the country is producing more goods and services than the year before.

Economic migrant: Someone who leaves his or her country to seek a more prosperous way of life.

The economy: all the organizations that provide goods and services, and all the individuals and organizations that buy them.

Editor: the person who is responsible for the content of a newspaper or television or radio programme.

Election: selection of one or more people for an official position by voting.

Electorate: all those registered to vote.

Emigration: leaving your homeland to move to another country.

Employment laws: laws passed by Parliament and by the EU that set out the rights and responsibilities of employers and employees.

Employment tribunal: a type of court that deals only with disagreements over employment laws.

Ethical: relating to a set of values including compassion, fairness, honesty, respect and responsibility.

Euro: the name of the single currency used by a group of countries within the European Union.

European Court of Human Rights: this court was set up to enforce the European Convention on Human Rights.

European ombudsman: a person who investigates complaints against the EU.

European Union (EU): a group of 25 countries that work together, for example on environmental, social and economic issues.

Fair Trade: a way of buying and selling products that aims to pay the producer a fair price.

First past the post: an electoral system where voters have one vote per constituency and the candidate with the most votes wins.

Forward Plan: a document that sets out the aims of a council in the long term.

Fossil fuel: a naturally occurring fuel, such as coal or natural gas.

Free trade: trade between countries that is not restricted by things like high taxes on imports.

General election: an election for a new government – at least every five years in the UK.

Geneva Convention: an internationally accepted set of rules on the treatment of people in war.

Genocide: mass murder of a racial, national or religious group.

Global warming: the rise in the average surface temperature of the Earth.

Globalization: the increasing interdependence of the world.

Government revenue: the money raised by the government.

Green Paper: puts forward ideas that the government wants discussed before it starts to develop policy.

Hereditary peers: people who inherited the title 'Lord' or 'Lady'.

High Court: the court where judges hear cases on serious crimes.

Homophobic: fearing or hating homosexuals.

House of Commons: the more powerful of the two parts of the British Parliament. Its members are elected by the public.

Human rights: things that people are morally or legally allowed to do or have.

Identity: who or what someone or something is.

Identity Card: a card that establishes someone's identity.

Immigration: moving to another country to live there.

Inclusive education: schooling that involves everyone, regardless of disability.

Inflation: the general rise in prices.

Interdependent: where businesses need each other to survive.

Interest: extra payment made to a lender by a borrower.

International Criminal Court: the Court that deals with the most serious crimes against humanity and with war crimes.

Journalist: a person who gathers news and produces reports for the media.

Judge: a person who decides questions of law in a court.

Judiciary: all the judges in a country.

Jury: a group of people who decide if someone is guilty in a court of law.

LEDC: a less economically developed country.

Legal rights: rights that are protected by law.

Libel: writing untrue things about people.

Lobby: to try to persuade MPs to support a particular point of view. This used to happen in the 'lobby', or hallway, on the way into Parliament.

Local Agenda 21: a global plan to ask local people how they think their immediate environment could be improved.

Magistrates' court: a court held before two or more public officers dealing with minor crimes.

Manifesto: a published statement of the aims and policies of a political party.

MEDC: a more economically developed country.

Media: ways of communicating with large numbers of people.

Member of Parliament: a person who has been elected to represent a part of the country in Parliament.

Member of the European Parliament: a person who has been elected to represent a part of the country in the European Parliament.

Member state: a country that is a member of the EU.

Minister of State: an assistant to the Secretary of State.

Minority: a small part of a larger group of people.

Minutes: a formal record of what has been said at a meeting.

Mitigating: making something less intense or severe.

Multicultural community: a community made up of people from many different cultural or ethnic groups.

Neighbourhood: a local area within which people live as neighbours, sharing living space and interests.

Office of Fair Trading: a government office that can take action against traders who break the law.

Ombudsman: a person who investigates complaints against the government or a public organization.

Opinion poll: questioning a sample of the population to build a picture of the views of the public on a particular topic.

Opposition: political parties who are not in power.

People's peers: people who are selected to sit in the House of Lords.

Political party: an organized group of people with common aims who put up candidates for elections.

Political rights: rights to take part in elections and other democratic activities.

Polling station: a place where votes are cast; often a school, library or village hall.

Postal vote: when voters make their vote by post, rather than by going to a polling station.

Poverty line: the income level below which someone cannot afford to live.

Press Code: guidelines for the media and journalists about the information they gather and how they obtain and use it.

Press freedom: the ability of the press to give information and express opinion.

Pressure groups: a group of people that tries to change public opinion or government policy to its own views or beliefs.

Prime Minister: the leader of the majority party in the House of Commons and the leader of the government.

Private sector: section of the economy made up of businesses or organizations that are owned by individuals or by shareholders.

Probation officer: someone who writes court reports on offenders and supervises them in the community.

Profit: money you gain when you sell something for more than you paid for it or than it cost to make.

Proportional representation: an electoral system in which the number of seats a party wins is roughly proportional to its national share of the vote.

Public consultation: involves asking the public about their opinions on changes in the law, policies or large-scale developments.

Public opinion: the popular view.

Public sector: section of the economy made up of organizations owned or run by the government and local councils.

Racism: the idea that some people of different origins are not as good as others.

Rate of inflation: the rate at which prices rise.

Recorder: a barrister or solicitor of at least ten years' experience, who acts as a part-time judge in a crown court.

Redistributing income: taking money from wealthier people through taxation, to give it to poorer people through benefits.

Redundancy: when a person loses their job because the job doesn't need to be done anymore.

Referendum: a vote by the whole electorate on a particular issue.

Refugee: a person who has been forced to leave their country and must live somewhere else.

Renewable: able to be replaced or restored.

Representative democracy: a type of democracy where citizens have the right to choose someone to represent them on a council or in Parliament.

Respect: to have a good opinion of someone.

Responsibility: something it is your duty to do or to look after.

Retraining: learning new skills that can be used in a different job.

School council: a group of people who represent the classes and year groups of the school. They give students the opportunity to participate in decision-making.

Secretary of State: an MP who is in charge of a government department such as health or defence.

Shadow Cabinet: MPs from the main opposition party who 'shadow' MPs who head major government departments.

Shareholder: someone who owns part of a business by owning shares in a company.

Single currency: this is the Euro, so called as it is used in some of the EU member states.

Slander: saying incorrect things about people.

Small claims court: a local court, which hears civil cases involving small amounts of money.

Solicitor: a lawyer who gives legal advice and may speak for their clients in court.

Specialised: where employees or businesses concentrate on tasks that they can do well.

Spin doctor: someone who tries to get certain stories into the public eye and to make bad news sound better.

Stakeholder: someone who has an interest in a decision that is being made.

Sue: to make a claim against someone or something.

Suffrage: the right to vote.

Suffragette: person who campaigned for the right of women to vote.

Sustainable communities: Places where social, economic and environmental activities form a community where people thrive both at home and at work.

Sustainable development: living now in a way that doesn't damage the needs of future generations.

Tolerant: open-minded, accepting.

Trade Unions: organizations that look after the interests of a group of employees.

Trading Standards Department: an official body that enforces consumer-based law.

United Nations: an international organization that tries to encourage peace, cooperation and friendship between countries.

Voluntary organizations: organizations with a social purpose, which do not aim to make a profit.

Volunteer: someone who works for free for a community.

Vote: to choose a candidate in an election.

Ward: an area that forms a separate part of a local council.

Warning: written or spoken warning given by an employer to an employee if the employer thinks the employee has been breaking the contract of employment.

White Paper: puts government policy up for discussion before it becomes law.

Youth Council: a group of young people who meet to discuss what is going on in the local area and put their ideas to the council.

Index

Answers to exam practice questions

Unit 1: Exam Section A

Theme 1

a) C

b) Two of: because human rights laws are being broken, because of racial or religious discrimination, because it is giving in to terrorists.

c) Race Relations Act, Equality Act.

d) B

e) Making travel more difficult for passengers by delaying everyone and the cost of installing scanning equipment means that 'the terrorists have won'.

f) He had not been properly trained.

g) D

h) To make up for the loss of his job.

i) A warning must be given.

j) Two of the following: negotiates with employers for pay/conditions; supports members when in dispute with employers; pushes for fairer legislation to protect employees.

Theme 2

a) i. Gordon Brown's getting desperate for votes.
   ii. More than 500,000 elderly patients are re-admitted to hospital each year.

b) Two of the following: the headline is biased; the first sentence gives an opinion that is against Brown; the last paragraph gives the Conservative point of view. There is nothing to support the Labour point of view.

c) A

d) A manifesto.

e) One of the following: tax, income tax, national insurance, VAT.

f) More people would take an interest in politics, and elections would be cheaper.

g) The proportion of people who vote in an election.

h) A referendum.

i) The UK is a democratic country, so by voting we have our say. If people don't vote, the country is not really democratic. A government can be voted in by a very small proportion of the population if people don't vote.

Theme 3

a) A

b) C

c) D

d) Two of the following: providing education and training, helping people to work, helping people to return to their homes by giving them skills.

e) Two of the following: being child soldiers, lacking education, being driven from their homes.

f) If people have no education or jobs, they cannot earn money to allow them to live a reasonable life. They are more likely to be ill and grow poorer and poorer. As education has to be paid for, they will not be able to afford education for the next generation.

g) Two of the following: trade; develop communications; encourage enterprise by lending money to people who want to run small businesses; develop health care, provide sustainable technology like water pumps.

The examiner will mark Section B by looking at both your skills and knowledge. The table below shows how. You need to look at both the levels and the possible content below to work out how well you have done. Because the questions are very open ended and can be approached in a variety of ways – the answers below give one way of looking at the question. If you have taken a different approach, work your way through the levels to see how you have done.

Level 0, Mark 0:

No answer or an answer that is totally irrelevant.

Level 1, Mark 1–3:

Opinion with little or no reasoning, showing simple knowledge and little understanding of issues and/or events. *There are some errors in spelling, punctuation and grammar but the basic meaning is clear.*

Level 2, Mark 4–6:

Mainly opinion with some reasoning, supported by limited relevant evidence and/or examples showing limited knowledge and some understanding of issues and/or events. Candidates who include only points for, or only points against are restricted to a maximum of 6 marks. *Spelling, punctuation and grammar are reasonably accurate and meaning is clear.*

Level 3, Mark 7–9:

Points **for** and **against** are included in a reasonably balanced and mostly reasoned discussion which shows quite good knowledge and understanding of issues and/or events, based on some evidence/argument. *Spelling, punctuation and grammar are mostly accurate and appropriate language is used to convey meaning.*

Level 4, Mark 10–12:

Points **for** and **against** are included in a balanced and reasoned discussion which shows good knowledge and understanding of issues and/or events, supported by strong evidence leading to a clear conclusion. *Fluent and consistently strong use of vocabulary and accurate spelling, punctuation and grammar with use of specialist terms.*

4   Your answer may look something like this.

The UK is multicultural because people of many races and religions live here. Some groups live and mix together well, but others keep to themselves and don't attempt to integrate with other groups.

People who have recently arrived in the UK often want to live with family and friends who come from the same area because they speak the same language and have the same customs. This makes them feel secure, as they may have arrived somewhere very different from their home country.

A multicultural country is more interesting because we share the cultures of many countries. For example, people flock to the 'China Town' districts in UK cities to enjoy the restaurants and the atmosphere of cultural events such as Chinese New Year.

Some immigrants are prepared to do jobs that people in the UK do not want to do. For example, there are many fruit pickers and other workers who come from other countries. Until these jobs were filled, farmers had been complaining that they couldn't find pickers and would need to plough the crops into the ground.

If different groups live separately, it can cause conflict. If people do not join in and appear very different, others may become suspicious or even afraid of them. Clearly, this can lead to difficulties. If people are living in the UK, it is important to learn to speak and write English so they can join in. When children go to school, they learn English but sometimes their parents do not speak the language. This makes it very difficult to take part in society.

Many new immigrants do learn to join in – but in some areas, some do not. They should be encouraged to do so. The government sets language standards for people who want to become British citizens to encourage them to learn English.

5   Your answer may look something like this.

We have laws so that people feel safe and all live by the same rules. We have rights and responsibilities but if some people take all their rights this can affect other people's lives. Laws set the limits on people's rights and protect people's freedoms. They tell us what our responsibilities are. Having a set of rules for everyone means that society works more smoothly.

Laws are made by Parliament – which is democratically elected, so we have all had a say in the laws that are passed. This should make us want to keep them. If laws were made by a dictator, it would be different because they would be imposed on us. This is one reason why it is important to vote.

People break the law for a variety of reasons. Some people do so to protest. Greenpeace breaks the law to get publicity for its environmental campaigns. This kind of protest can be disruptive but aims not to cause actual harm. Some other protesters do really harmful things. Some animal rights protestors do things that might hurt people. In America, anti-abortionists have killed some doctors who perform abortions.

Sometimes people break the law in less serious ways. If they need to take someone to hospital urgently, they might break the speed limit. Usually if they explain, they are let off. This is known as mitigating circumstances.

People also break the law because they want to change a law. This is linked to the motive of protest – but that is not always to change the law. Sometimes laws are not perfect and try to enforce rules that large numbers of people do not agree with. If this is really the case, breaking the law could be justified but it would be better to use one of the legal ways of bringing about change.

6 Your answer may look something like this.

Global warming is considered to be a problem because it will change the way we live. It will make life more difficult for many people. For example, parts of Africa will become desert and other areas, like Bangladesh, will be flooded if sea levels rise. It will also affect the

UK because the weather gets stormier and we have more floods.

The government uses all sorts of ways to encourage people to reduce carbon emissions, which are thought to be the cause of global warming. The EU sets targets that the UK government uses as its benchmark for its own targets – which are generally higher. Most of the targets for individuals are designed to encourage us to do something, rather than make us do it. Businesses are treated more strictly and can be fined if they break the pollution limits.

The government finds it hard to make individuals obey laws. For example, to cut down on rubbish by law it would mean checking every wheelie bin to see what people are throwing away. There have been suggestions that microchips should be put on bins to check on people's waste but so far this hasn't worked. The government has done some things like banning 100-watt light bulbs so people have to use energy-efficient bulbs. Success therefore depends on goodwill.

It is therefore clear that we have a responsibility to look after the environment. The government cannot do it alone. If the earth is to be sustainable, we must make sure that we do not damage it for future generations. This means that we must take responsibility for doing whatever we can to reduce our individual carbon footprint. This might mean using public transport when we can, recycling our waste whenever possible and buying things that have less packaging and are sustainably produced.

Unit 3 Citizenship in Context

Option A
Environmental change and sustainable development

1 B

2 D

3 C

4 A

5 B

6 B

7 D

8 China's population is very large, so the total emissions are high. However, individually people do not produce very much carbon dioxide, so the output per head is low.

9 As nuclear power stations do not produce carbon dioxide, they help to slow the growth of our output of CO_2 produced from other sources.

10 Bee-keeping will give people an income that will help them to farm more effectively and sell more crops. They will then be able to buy more things for their families and send their children to school. All these things will help the economy to grow, which will increase trade.

11 Aid can either meet the needs of people in emergencies or provide continuing food aid to keep people going. It can also help countries to develop. This might mean education and training or helping a country to build roads and ports. It is better to give development aid so the economy of the country can grow and people can become better off. When people learn skills, they can earn a better living and improve their family's future.

12 a) Two of: in order to reduce the output of CO_2; to protect the environment for the future; to reduce global warming.

   b) Two of: LEDCS don't want development slowed down; it will cost more to produce things if they have to cut carbon emissions; MEDCs were able to develop at a time when they did not have to be concerned about carbon emissions.

13 a) The rise in the average surface temperature of the earth.

   b) Two of: increasing the amount of greenhouse gases in the atmosphere; global changes to the land surface such as deforestation; increasing concentration of aerosols in the atmosphere.

14 When you read the points below you should also refer to the levels tables at the end of the Workbook. These show the scores you can achieve in the exam for the quality of your argument.

   Points in favour of taxation and regulation:
   • People are more prepared to take it seriously if they have to pay.
   • Most people won't make the effort if there is no penalty.
   • The country is more likely to achieve its targets if there are laws about it.

   Points against taxation and regulation:
   • It is difficult to achieve results with persuasion.
   • If there are penalties and taxes people will just dump rubbish at the roadside instead of paying the price of having refuse removed.
   • It is only fair if every country does it, because it will make everything that is made here cost more, so the price of UK-produced goods will rise.

15 When you read the points below you should also refer to the levels tables at the end of the Workbook. These show the scores you can achieve in the exam for the quality of your argument.

Points in favour of 'looking after the environment is important':
• We must be sustainable in the long run – even if scientists argue about the causes of global warming.
• We need to work out the best way to achieve targets for CO_2 reduction.
• Some methods of reducing outputs of carbon dioxide might help more people than they harm so they should go ahead.
• When decisions have been made democratically, there should be no argument about their implementation.

Points in favour of 'individuals' rights are important':
• Pressure groups may have loud voices and individuals' rights may be ignored.
• People's human rights must be respected.
• People will complain about developments because they do not want their own environment to be destroyed.
• People who live in cities might not understand the value of the countryside.

Option B
Changing communities: social and cultural identities

1 D

2 B

3 C

4 A

5 C

6 D

7 A

8 Two of: by lining the streets; by standing in silence, by stopping the usual activities of the town.

9 Three of: Sex Discrimination Act; Race Relations Act; Disability Discrimination Act; employment legislation, which covers discrimination on grounds of sex, age or religion.

10 Two of: joining celebrations; learning languages; cooking food from other cultures; joining groups with diversity.

11 Points could include the following or other reasonable suggestions: organise events to celebrate the cultural mix; support language lessons; educate the community; encourage people to integrate; encourage parents to

participate in school events. In each case you should give reasons for why you think it would be effective. You should also indicate which ways you think would be the most effective.

12 a) An asylum seeker is someone who has applied for protection as a refugee and is fleeing persecution.

An economic migrant is someone who leaves their country to seek a more prosperous way of life.

b) A points-based system is used when assessing whether or not to allow people into the UK. The system requires proof from asylum seekers.

13 a) A group of people that tries to change public opinion or government policy to be in line with its own views or beliefs and so to help achieve its aims.

b) A political party has policies that cover all aspects of the country and economy. A pressure group is usually concerned with a single issue like the environment, children or health.

14 This is a question of community versus environment. Refer to the levels tables at the end of the Workbook to help you measure the quality of your argument.

In favour of pulling down Toxteth Street:
- New houses would be energy efficient.
- New houses would be cheaper to run.
- The area would be given a 'new start' by being rebuilt.

In favour of saving Toxteth Street:
- There is a strong community, which would be lost.
- The community is distinctive.
- People feel safe.
- People look after each other.
- The pressure group also claims it would be cheaper to refurbish and less CO_2 would be released.

15 Refer to the levels tables at the end of the Workbook to help you measure the quality of your argument.

Arguments in favour:
- If everyone is integrated, people may lose their language, traditions and religion.
- The UK may lose its own culture and identity.

Arguments against:
- People will understand each other better.

- Increased community cohesion.
- There will be more job opportunities for people who learn/speak English and therefore a more equal society.
- The mix of cultures is already embedded and many people enjoy the new experiences of different cultures.

Option C
Influencing and changing decisions in society and government

1 B

2 A

3 C

4 D

5 C

6 D

7 D

8 Two of the following: to help people; to improve things; to support an important cause; because they want to use their spare time in a useful way; to meet people; to learn new skills; because of their religious beliefs; to give something back to society.

9 Two of the following: income tax; VAT; national insurance; corporation tax; inheritance tax.

10 Two of the following:
- They could write to or lobby their local MP or councillors, who should take an interest because of the local connection.
- They could contact the local/national media to raise interest in the local/national community.
- They could hold meetings to bring the community together.

11 Three different reasons and explanations:
- Being in prison means you don't have much contact with family and friends, so it is difficult to feel 'at home' on leaving.
- It makes it hard to get a job, therefore people may go back to crime to make a living.
- Poor education in prison – many have poor qualifications on entering and need to improve to get a job.
- In prison, people aren't used to being in a work environment, so it can be difficult to keep to the routine of a job when try to make a life outside prison.
- There are many things in life that we have to organize for ourselves. In prison, daily life is set

out, and arrangements are taken care of, so on leaving it can be hard to manage all kinds of things (like getting benefits, paying taxes and paying bills).

12 a) Two of the following: directly through government changing the law; through the media; through opinion polls carried out by pressure groups.

b) One of the following with explanation: small sample, therefore not very representative; respondents likely to have strong views; people sometimes give the answer they think people will want to hear, so not accurate.

13 a) One of the following: trying to be popular so that it will be re-elected; deciding that some things are more important than others.

b) The government is responsible for its actions and must be able to explain them to the voters.

14 Refer to the levels tables at the end of the Workbook to help you measure the quality of your argument.

Arguments in favour of voting at 16:

- You pay taxes and can work, fight for your country and get married at 16, so should be able to decide on the party that makes the decisions that affect you.
- It might increase young people's interest in political decisions.
- Young people are maturing earlier.
- Citizenship education means young people are better informed.
- The government might consider young people more if they have to think about winning their vote.

Arguments against voting at 16:

- People have not enough experience of the world at 16.
- They might be too easily biased.
- The turnout of 18-year-old voters is low – so might be a waste of time.

15 Refer to the levels tables at the end of the Workbook to help you measure the quality of your argument.

Arguments in favour of the statement:

- The United Nations Declaration on Human Rights protects our privacy and civil liberties.
- The UN and EU have fought to protect our human rights and it is part of UK law.
- The UK government has been breaking the EU Convention on Human Rights by keeping DNA collected from innocent people. It has been told to stop.
- It also wants to make sure that all emails are saved and can be checked in case people are breaking the law.
- Laws that have reduced our freedoms to protect us from terrorism have been used to convict people for other offences.

Arguments against the statement:

- We must do all we can to protect people from terrorism, so the government is entitled to reduce our civil liberties.
- The government needs to know what we are doing and where we are going so it can plan how to keep us safe.
- For example, identity cards will help the government with such information.

Assessment objectives and levels

Assessment objectives

The examiners use these assessment objectives when they are assessing Unit 1 and Unit 3. (AO2 is mainly assessed through the controlled assessment in Units 2 and 4.)

AO1 26%	Recall, select and communicate their knowledge and understanding of citizenship concepts, issues and terminology.
AO2 44%	Apply skills, knowledge and understanding when planning, taking and evaluating citizenship actions in a variety of contexts.
AO3 30%	Analyse and evaluate issues and evidence including different viewpoints to construct reasoned arguments and draw conclusion.

Assessment levels

You can use these tables to help you achieve the highest marks possible. Look at the descriptor for the highest marks, then in your answer try to do everything that the descriptor says.

So, for example, if you want to get high marks in a 6-mark question, you will need to include 'three or more well-chosen points supported by simple but acceptable examples or evidence.'

Assessment levels for 6-mark questions in Unit 3

Level	Mark	Descriptor
0	0	The answer does not seriously address the question.
1	1–2	The answer offers just 1 or 2 very simple points only without any development.
2	3–4	The answer makes two or three points but they are fairly superficial and any examples will probably be generalised.
3	5–6	**Three or more well-chosen points supported by simple but acceptable examples or evidence.**

Assessment levels for 8-mark questions in Unit 3

Level	Mark	Descriptor
0	0	No rewardable material.
1	1–2	Basic and/or very brief approach relying on opinion with basic knowledge and little understanding of the issue.
2	3–4	An approach which relies mainly on opinion but with limited relevant evidence and some knowledge and understanding of the issue.
3	5–6	Students who give only one point of view (either 'for' or 'against' fortnightly collections, are limited to a maximum of 4 marks. An approach covering both points of view and which uses some evidence to develop limited arguments and demonstrates quite good knowledge and understanding.
4	7–8	A balanced approach covering both points of view on fortnightly collections and which uses clear evidence to support arguments and demonstrates good knowledge and understanding.

Assessment levels for 12-mark questions in Unit 1

Level	Mark	Descriptor
0	0	No rewardable material.
1	1–3	Opinion with little or no reasoning, showing simple knowledge and little understanding of issues and/or events. *There are some errors in spelling, punctuation and grammar but the basic meaning is clear.*
2	4–6	Mainly opinion with some reasoning, supported by limited relevant evidence and/or examples showing limited knowledge and some understanding of issues and/or events. Candidates who include **only** points for, or **only** points against are restricted to a maximum of 6 marks. *Spelling, punctuation and grammar are reasonably accurate and meaning is clear.*
3	7–9	Points **for** and **against** are included in a reasonably balanced and mostly reasoned discussion which shows quite good knowledge and understanding of issues and/or events, based on some evidence/argument. *Spelling, punctuation and grammar are mostly accurate and appropriate language is used to convey meaning.*
4	10–12	Points **for** and **against** are included in a balanced and reasoned discussion which shows good knowledge and understanding of issues and/or events, supported by strong evidence leading to a clear conclusion. *Fluent and consistently strong use of vocabulary and accurate spelling, punctuation and grammar with use of specialist terms.*

Assessment levels for 15-mark Questions in Unit 3

Level	Mark	Descriptor
0	0	No rewardable material
1	1–3	Opinion with little or no reasoning, showing simple knowledge and little understanding of issues and/or events. *There are some errors in spelling, punctuation and grammar but the basic meaning is clear.*
2	4–6	Opinion with limited reasoning, supported by limited relevant evidence and/or examples showing basic knowledge and understanding of issues and/or events. Students who include **only** points for, or **only** points against are restricted to a maximum of 6 marks. *Spelling, punctuation and grammar are reasonably accurate and meaning is clear.*
3	7–9	Points **for** and **against** are included in a simple but reasonably effective discussion which shows some knowledge and understanding of some issues and/or events. *Spelling, punctuation and grammar are mostly accurate and appropriate language is used to convey meaning.*
4	10–12	Points **for** and **against** are included in a mainly balanced and reasoned discussion which shows quite good knowledge and understanding of issues and/or events, based on evidence/argument and leading towards a conclusion. *Spelling, punctuation and grammar are accurate and appropriate language is used together with some use of specialist terms.*
5	13–15	Points **for** and **against** are included in a balanced, reasoned and coherent discussion which shows good knowledge and understanding of issues and/or events, supported by strong evidence and arguments leading to a reasoned conclusion. *Fluent and consistently strong use of vocabulary and accurate spelling, punctuation and grammar with use of specialist terms.*